On Active Service with the Chinese Regiment

The memorial stone on the road leading to the new barracks at Matou, Wei-hai-wei.

ON ACTIVE SERVICE WITH THE CHINESE REGIMENT

A RECORD OF THE OPERATIONS OF THE FIRST CHINESE REGIMENT IN NORTH CHINA FROM MARCH TO OCTOBER 1900. BY CAPTAIN A. A. S. BARNES

D1612514

The Naval & Military Press Ltd

in association with

The National Army Museum, London

Published jointly by

The Naval & Military Press Ltd
Unit 10 Ridgewood Industrial Park,
Uckfield, East Sussex,
TN22 5QE England

Tel: +44 (0) 1825 749494
Fax: +44 (0) 1825 765701

www.naval-military-press.com
www.military-genealogy.com
www.militarymaproom.com

and

The National Army Museum, London
www.national-army-museum.ac.uk

CONTENTS

vii

CONTENTS

PART V.—IN PEKING

PART VI.—OTHER OPERATIONS

PART VII.—ON THE LINES OF COMMUNICATION

LIST OF ILLUSTRATIONS

PLANS

INTRODUCTION

EVERY book, more or less, is written with an object of some sort, and this little one is no exception to this general rule.

So many unkind things have been said about the Chinese regiment, by people with no knowledge of the matter, that it has seemed advisable to place on record the doings of the regiment on service, in the real hard fighting in Northern China in 1900, as they actually occurred, in order to show that, though a regiment in its extreme infancy, fighting, under alien officers and for an alien cause, against its own compatriots, its own Emperor, and his Imperial troops, it bore its part with the best, deserving none of the somewhat nasty things that have been put abroad about it; but, on the other hand, more than fulfilling the high hopes formed of it by its officers, and by those in high military authority who caused its formation.

People, moreover, with memories of remarkable brevity have, to all appearances, quite forgotten that the regiment saw any fighting at all. The memories of these will, I trust, be refreshed, both by my own contributions, and by those of others set out in the Appendices attached hereto. The various cuttings referred to possibly form the most valuable part of the book, for they, at all events, can claim absolute impartiality—a virtue that I am naturally only able to strive after, with indifferent success. Historically, I can claim that all related herein as to the doings of the Chinese regiment is correct so far as anything can humanly be, and that is, after all, the main point.

I regret to see my own name and the first person singular appear so very often, but when one is only setting down what one saw, or did, or saw done one's self, it is hard to see how this can be avoided. I have sought for, and obtained, much assistance from others who were where I was not, and saw what I did not see, so that I hope no one who was anywhere where things were stirring will find that important fact omitted. I can only say that I have tried my best to get the fullest details of all the "Shows," great and small, in which the regiment was represented, and if I have failed in any particular I must plead Not Guilty of intent.

If I seem to anyone unduly optimistic about the work done by our men during those trying times, I can only say that my views are fully shared by those who had the same chances of judging as I had, and that, in these matters, seeing is believing.

It will be seen, from a perusal of these pages, that, as a unit, the Chinese regiment was represented in more expeditions than any other corps. To say nothing of the original troubles round Wei-hai-wei, we had our part in Tientsin, the relief of Peking, and the smaller expeditions, on the 19th August 1900, that to Tu Liu, and the abortive one to Peitsang. No other regiment was represented in all these. In the Paoting-fu expedition, it is true, we took no part, as we had then returned to our own place, Wei-hai-wei; but we were, all the same, represented by Captain Brooke, who was signalling officer to the force from Tientsin.

Other corps, raised by our countrymen from more or less promising material, have proved their worth in the day of trial; but I do not believe anyone has had to undergo its baptism of fire in conditions and amid surroundings so hard as had the Chinese regiment. Our officers have led aliens against their own races often and often in our national history, but I doubt if the circumstances were ever before such as they were in North China in 1900. Our enemy was no mean one; he was well armed, well provided with artillery, and in every way our equal, except, of course, in the important matter of officers. He had fanaticism, religion, and pride, three of the strongest incentives to war, on his side, and if he lacked patriotism, as we know it, he possessed it, indirectly, in his hatred of, and his contempt for, all foreigners.

The Chinese, as a soldier, has many sterling qualities. He is very amenable to the discipline and control of those he knows; he is stout and well able to stand fatigue and hard work; he is a very good shot, taken all round; is no trouble to feed, as he has no prejudices on the subject, except it be in the matter of quantity; and, as I have endeavoured to show, he is good on service, whether on the actual field, or on those more frequent duties of a more peaceful and less exciting nature that fall to a soldier's lot at such times.

It may be asked how the excellence which I have ascribed to the Chinese regiment is to be accounted for, and here, of course, I can only give my own opinion, which is, that the behaviour of the men was due simply and solely to the steady drill all the recruits had, and have, to undergo. I am well aware that this same steady drill is regarded in some circles as old-fashioned and out-of-date, but without it, I am sure, no regiment of Chinese will ever succeed, whatever may be the case with other organisations more or less similar.

I have already referred to the assistance I have

received from others with regard to matters outside my own personal knowledge, and I take this opportunity of thanking those to whom I am chiefly indebted — namely, Captains Watson, Toke, Bray, and Brooke, and Mr Schaller, for much valuable help.

A. A. S. BARNES.

WEI-HAI-WEI,
13th October 1901.

ON ACTIVE SERVICE WITH THE CHINESE REGIMENT

PART I

THE TROUBLES ROUND WEI-HAI-WEI

CHAPTER I

WHO or what was responsible I do not consider it within my province to inquire, or even to conjecture, but certain it is that early in 1900, when all was quiet in other parts of China, the inhabitants of our territory round Wei-hai-wei were deeply affected with that bitter anti-foreign feeling which, later in the year, led to the Boxer rising, and its subsequent acts of war.

As soon as the approach of more clement weather made such things possible—to wit, early in March of that year—gatherings, whose sole and avowed object was the expulsion of the British, began to take place in two, if not three, sections of the territory, some two or three thousand men of all ages attending at each centre, on the average. The local village militia, or trained bands, were

A

also called out, incense was burned, flags erected, arms dug out or bought, and things began, generally, to look lively.

Rumours of these goings-on naturally reached the ears of the authorities, and it was determined to nip the thing in the bud. Accordingly, on the 26th of March, information having previously reached him, Colonel Bower struck what was probably the first blow of a long series which China has since been dealt, to show her that the Western barbarian has come to stay. With no hint to anyone, the available men of the regiment, to the number of some 420, paraded at the usual hour, received ten rounds of ball ammunition per man, and started out along the road to Chefoo. At a temple, some five or six miles out, was found a gathering of some six or seven hundred men, who showed no signs whatever of enmity, but allowed the regiment to march through them, and quietly surround them. The ringleaders were then invited to come to the front and account for themselves. One of them requested Colonel Bower to dismount before he deigned to enter into conversation, but, needless to say, the Colonel remained mounted. Some of the more truculent members of the mob now began to shout and make those noises peculiar to all such assemblies, and, for a few minutes, things looked decidedly dangerous. A most timely order, however, to fix bayonets, promptly carried out, turned the tide in favour of peace, and was at once followed by another to set about disarming the malcontents. A more weird collection has seldom been seen. There were a few more modern firearms, a large number of old matchlocks, all loaded with shot and slugs, but by far the greater number of these misguided peasants were content with sticks with old knives or bayonets lashed to one end, pitchforks, and other implements of peace rather than war. There were also three or four rusty old cannon, a big drum, and a telescopic trumpet, besides rough spears. In several cases the warriors were content with rifle barrels, which, no doubt, they thought contained all the virtues of the complete article. Three prisoners were then selected, including the gentleman who asked the Colonel to dismount, and the regiment returned to its barracks at Matou, laden with the somewhat cumbersome spoils of war.

Trivial and bloodless as this, the regiment's first real test, may seem, a little reflection will prove that it was really of vast importance, as being the first indication of what was afterwards so often and so abundantly shown—namely, the readiness of the men to stand by their officers, even against their own people.

CHAPTER II

Iᴛ has always struck me how providentially the initiation of the Chinese regiment into the actual mysteries of active service has been carried out. We began, as has been already recounted, with an absolutely bloodless, and almost friendly, dispersal of an unlawful gathering. At the time, there was not an officer, down to the latest arrival, who was not proud of the men, and of their behaviour on the occasion in question, or who was not as sure as could be that they could be fully relied on for sterner work, should the occasion arise. None, however, had any idea how close was the sterner work.

After the occurrence already related, things at once resumed their normal state, and the drilling of the recruit proceeded as it had done for the last year. It is curious, however, that just about this time (March 1900) we began to hear rumours of probable concerted action by the Powers, owing to the disturbed state of the country round Tientsin, and about the middle of the following month we had rumours that the said Powers had sent China an ultimatum on the "Boxer" business. It is also

noteworthy that on Easter Saturday, April 14th,
a Chinese cruiser arrived with the Taotai for the
Wei-hai-wei Boundary Commission on board, and
fired no salute, which omission caused some comment at the time.

On the 25th April the long-delayed Boundary
Commission started. It consisted of Colonel Bower,
Major Penrose, R.E., and Mr Schaller, Colonel
Bower's Chinese Secretary, on our part, and of
Taotais Li and Yen, and Captain Lin, Chinese
Navy, on the part of China. The escort was found
by No. 7 Company, under Captain Pereira, with
Lieutenant Brooke and Colour-Sergeant Brook,
and numbering some sixty men. Owing to some
appearance of hostility on the part of the in-
habitants, who had got some most extraordinary
ideas as to the true inwardness of the Commission,
No. 1 Company, under Lieutenant Toke, was sent
out on the 30th to strengthen the escort.

That same evening, when the officers were at
dinner, a message came from Major Bruce, who
was in command in the absence of the Colonel,
that he wanted to see all the officers at 9.30 P.M.
He then announced that the Boundary Commission
was in danger, and that he was going to their
assistance at once. Accordingly, at 1 A.M. the men
were roused, and at 3 A.M. Nos. 2, 4, and 5 Companies, about 170 strong, started for the camp at

Tsao-miao-tze, about eighteen miles due south. Arriving about 9.30 A.M., we found all quiet, and no immediate danger to be looked for. The following morning the Boundary Commission, with its escort further reinforced by some of No. 5 Company, moved on, No. 2 and the rest of No. 5 returned to barracks, while No. 4 remained at Tsao-miao-tze as a sort of precaution.

It is impossible to leave this little scare without a word as to the behaviour of the men. Roused from their sleep at the dead of night and ordered to march out, armed and equipped, against their own people, by alien officers, not a murmur was heard, and not a man was there but showed the greatest zeal. On that long march, too, and in all the discomforts of the bivouac at its end, their cheerful alacrity and discipline were right good to behold. It is impossible to imagine any troops behaving better, and giving less trouble—in fact, they gave none at all. This we may safely call their second test—not a great one, perhaps, but still a test.

Things remained in what one can best describe as a neutral state, until Saturday the 5th May, when, as Major Penrose, R.E., was out at work on the boundary delimitation, accompanied by two of his own corps, Mr Schaller, and twelve men of the regiment, the party was suddenly attacked by a large crowd of Chinese, armed chiefly with agricultural implements and stones. Major Penrose was the main objective, and he was very severely handled, especially with a bayonet, wrested from him, and which he had taken from one of the escort after emptying his own revolver into the mob. Sergeant Pillay and the other man of the Royal Engineers also put in some good work with their pistols, while Mr Schaller formed up the escort, and kept the crowd off Major Penrose, who had, by that time, fallen. Things now began to look very serious, for the crowd, though losing rapidly, showed no signs of giving way. Individuals, possibly imbued with Boxer notions of invulnerability, repeatedly tried to come to close quarters again, after once being driven back, several with more than one bullet in their bodies.

It should be mentioned that the attack first took place in a dry river-bed, along which the party was proceeding on its way back to camp. As soon as things began to look serious they withdrew up the hill on the right of their track, and still maintained a running fight in the direction of the camp, about half-a-mile off. The Chinese had allowed for this, and a large number now appeared above the party, and began to throw great stones at them. Several were shot

while so employed, and the attack began to lose
some of the *élan* which had at first been its
chief feature. The danger was, however, by no
means over, for the ammunition of the party was
fast running out, when the welcome "hiss-hiss"
of bullets was heard, and assistance was seen to
be coming from the camp. The mob now made
off the best way they could, but not before a
good few more were shot.

Let us now turn to the people in the camp,
and see, as well as we can, how the affray looked
to them. About 2 P.M. the "Alarm" was sounded
by the bugler on duty, who had luckily seen the
attack commence. The companies in camp, Nos.
1 and 7, at once fell in, and ammunition was
issued to them. Following their officers, Colonel
Bower, Captain Pereira, and Lieutenant Toke,
they started at the double for the fight. Some
firing also took place, but not much, as it was
impossible in the press to see who was who.
However, the mob started to run, and some of
the men, headed by Captain Pereira, rushed after
them. A few turned back, and one put his
pitchfork round Captain Pereira's neck, and bore
him to the ground, where he would have fared
but ill had not one of his men, who was close
behind him, bayoneted his assailant.

Meantime, some fire was opened from the left

of the two companies, and a fresh crowd was
seen coming round the side of the hill on which
was Major Penrose's party, with the evident
intention of getting between it and the camp.
A few volleys, however, soon had the desired
effect, and it, too, dispersed. In this affair, Major
Penrose was severely wounded, Sergeant Pillay
was cut about the face, Captain Pereira was
slightly injured, and two men of No. 7 Company
were very badly knocked about with sticks and
stones. One of the latter, who belonged to the
escort, fell down off the hill to which his party
withdrew, among the mob, and, in addition to his
injuries, had his rifle and bayonet taken from
him. The Chinese left twenty dead on the field,
but it could not be ascertained how many were
wounded, though the number could not have
been few.

This attack, disastrous as it was to its originators,
and, not impossibly, to many who had come out as
spectators and with the amiable intention of joining
in the spoiling of the " foreign devils " had they
been overcome, was the first actual occasion on
which the regiment had been " blooded," so to say ;
and it must be admitted that their behaviour all
through was simply grand, especially that of the
escort to Major Penrose, but for whose staunchness
that officer and the other Europeans with him,

might easily have lost their lives. It is impossible to withhold all praise from these men, or from that brave man to whose ready bayonet Captain Pereira possibly owes his life. No other soldiers could have done better; many might have done worse.

It is a fortunate thing that this attack did not take place at a greater distance from the camp, as might easily have been the case, seeing that the party had, at one time, been at least six miles away. Had this been done, the party might have been wiped out before it was even known in camp that they were in danger. For some days, the natives had shown an almost friendly and quite peaceful disposition, which accounts for the smallness of the escort, which, up till then, had consisted of an officer and thirty men, but it is not impossible that the Chinese had counted on this, or, at least, had observed the diminution of the escort, and taken advantage of it.

Whether this attack, and the general unrest in the territory which was apparent at this time, had any close connection with the anti-foreign rising farther north, is a matter of doubt, and the general consensus of opinion is that the two were quite distinct, the fact that the local outbreak occurred at that particular time being merely a coincidence. This view is a good deal borne out by the most peaceful attitude of the inhabitants later on, when

Matou was occupied by only some fifty recruits, owing to the bulk of the regiment being at the front. At all events, it was a grand thing for the regiment, as it showed the officers that their hard work had borne the best of fruit; and, what is possibly more important, it proved the value of the regiment to others, and enabled us to justify our existence.

Let us now return to Captain Watson, whom we left with Lieutenant Bray, Colour-Sergeant Purdon, and No. 4 Company, some sixty strong, in camp at Tsao-miao-tze.

On the 5th of May they were warned by Colonel Bower of the attack on Major Penrose and his party, and told to be on the lookout. The following morning the two officers rode to the hills west of the camp, instead of sending a patrol, as had been the custom. On reaching the high ground they saw large numbers of people advancing in the direction of the camp. Captain Watson went on a little, and on getting on to the next bit of rising ground, found that there was a large crowd about 600 yards from him, who, as soon as they saw him, set up a terrific yell. The estimated numbers of these misguided people was about 3000. The officers galloped back to the camp, fell in their men, and issued extra ammunition. This was at 11.15 A.M. By 11.30 the semicircle of hills facing the camp on the north, west, and south was covered with Chinese, who commenced to wave their weapons and shout. The company was about to move out to meet the impending attack, when an old man, apparently carrying all his worldly goods on a stick over his shoulder, was seen running towards the camp. He turned out to be the father of one of the men, and he had come to warn his son that thousands were on their way to wipe out the camp and all in it, and that if his son had any regard for his own skin he would get out as soon as he could. The son replied that if there was going to be a fight he preferred to remain where he was. The old man continued his flight through the camp alone.

The mob was all this time closing in, so Captain Watson moved out with half the company towards the south-west, while Lieutenant Bray held the rising ground above the camp on the north side. Firing now commenced on both sides, and the result of our men's fire was that two or three of the mob were brought down. This caused them some little surprise, and created some excitement, at the same time checking the ardour of the advance. After considering the fallen for some time the mob came on once more, and our fire was continued until they finally stopped, broke, and then fled in all directions.

Their fire was more remarkable for its noise

Captain Watson's camp at Tsao-miao-tze. The attack of 6th of May 1900 was made from the hills in the background.

than for any effect it had. Bullets, slugs, nails, and odd bits of metal fell around in profusion, but with no harm to any of our people. On their right flank the mob had a wonderful piece of ordnance, carried by several men. It made a terrific noise and emitted an immense volume of smoke, but no projectile ever seemed to come out of it. If one ever did it must either have fallen very short or gone far over the camp, most likely the former, as nothing was ever seen or heard of it. After about an hour of this the hills were cleared, and the men were withdrawn into the camp. They had hardly done so when a small crowd was seen collecting on the south side, above Tsao-miao-tze. Captain Watson ordered Colour-Sergeant Purdon to fire one shot at them, as a hint to go away. The bullet struck the ground close to an old man, who thereupon opened an old umbrella and made off as hard as he could, under the impression, no doubt, that it afforded him ample cover in case of another shot. These misguided peasants were said to have had some twenty men killed, and more wounded, but, as the fallen were taken away, there was no chance at the time to ascertain exactly what losses they had actually sustained. On our side the losses were *nil*.

CHAPTER III

It should be mentioned that on the 1st of May, when Major Bruce proceeded to reinforce Colonel Bower's party, a supply camp had been established at Yang-chia-tang, in the south corner of the bay, consisting of No. 3 Company, which had remained there.

On Sunday morning, the 6th May, in consequence of the attack on Major Penrose and party, No. 2 Company was ordered out to the supply camp, to be ready to proceed inland when and where needed. It was warned at 9 A.M., and started at 10.50, which shows that the Chinese soldier does not take long to get under way. Meantime came the news of the attack on Captain Watson's camp at Tsao-miao-tze on the same day, so this company was sent off the following morning to either reinforce, relieve, or, possibly, avenge No. 4, as it was quite impossible to even conjecture what further developments might have taken place after the first attack, no news having been received. At the same time, No. 6 was sent out direct from Matou Barracks to reinforce the Colonel's escort. Neither of these companies met with any resistance, but several small gatherings

14

were seen *en route*, which at once dispersed, and, in
several cases, individuals and small parties were
come upon unawares, armed with sticks, iron bars,
and other seemingly unnecessary weapons. It will
be apparent, however, that the march of these small
bodies, through a country full of hostile natives, was
not without its excitements, the more so as neither
of the officers in command knew in the least what
he might be called upon to do at the end of his
journey. As it turned out, however, all was quiet
at both points. At the same time, these marches,
peaceful as they were, were still another test of
the men.

For the next day or two the interest is centred
round the camp at Tsao-miao-tze, formed of Nos. 2
and 4 Companies. It must be stated that for a
week or more the Chinese Commissioners had been
held prisoners—possibly not all unwillingly—at a
village, in Chinese territory, called Taotou, about
two miles to the south-west of Tsao-miao-tze, and
about this time the Governor of Shantung wired to
Colonel Dorward, the Commissioner, to effect their
release. On the afternoon of the 8th May, accordingly, Major Bruce arrived with 100 Marines to
strengthen the two companies of the regiment, for
this purpose. Leaving the Marines in reserve on
the high ground overlooking both villages, he proceeded with the two companies to Taotou to inter-

view the prisoners and set them free. He found
them most singularly averse to availing themselves
of his kindness, although their gaolers had fled.
However, their coyness was of no avail, for they
were ordered to be ready at 10 A.M. next day, to
be conducted to Colonel Bower's camp.

The next day, accordingly, the same plan was
adopted, and this time the Taotai and his fellow-
Commissioners met the party. They were at once
handed over to No. 2 Company, Captain Barnes
having orders to conduct them to Colonel Bower's
camp, about thirteen miles away.   Just at that
moment a regiment of Chinese troops was seen
approaching from the west, and, as it was uncertain
on what errand they had come, the Marines were
hurried down towards Taotou, and the Taotai and
his following in the opposite direction. However,
it was soon apparent that Colonel Wang and his men
had come, too late, to do what had just been done—
viz. release the Taotai; so, after expressions of
mutual good feeling, the two forces separated,
Colonel Wang returning to Chefoo.

No. 2 left Tsao-miao-tze at 11.15 A.M., and arrived
at Colonel Bower's camp at 2.45 P.M., at which hour
the Commissioners were safely delivered over.   On
the return journey, this company left at 4.40 P.M. and
reached Tsao-miao-tze at 7.30, which, considering
the distance, the hilly nature of the country, and

other circumstances, shows that the Chinese can march, in addition to the other military attributes it is the main object of these pages to show they possess.

After the incidents already recorded, all was more or less peace, but still another test was to be applied to our men. Finding, to all appearances, that force was of no avail, the Chinese tried another way to render the regiment at all events less of a thorn in their sides. A proclamation was issued to the effect that all of our men from the district, who did not return to their homes, and leave us to our fate, by a certain date, would have those same homes destroyed, and their nearest relatives punished, if not killed. To their eternal credit be it recorded that not one man can be said to have been enticed away on this plea, although many came to their officers to know if they could rely on the long arm of England seeing them righted in case any of these threatened misfortunes overtook their homes. So far as is known, this threat seems to have been largely "bluff," but anyone who knows what a strong characteristic of the Chinese home and paternal affection is, will realise that the test to the men's loyalty was no mean one.

There were not a few instances of individual loyalty, of which one or two deserve to be recorded. A man of No. 2 Company who was on pass near Colonel Bower's camp, hearing that

B

trouble was brewing, hastened to warn that officer, who directed him to rejoin his company. Thinking it was still at Matou, the man hastened there, only to find it gone out to Tsao-miao-tze. Thither he followed it, more or less in disguise, it being unhealthy for single men of the regiment to go far out, having travelled some forty miles in twenty-four hours, when it was clearly to his interest to remain quietly at home till he saw which way the cat meant to jump. Two men of No. 7 Company were in a village near the Colonel's camp before the attack on Major Penrose, and were taken prisoners and bound up. All the able-bodied in the village then went off to join in the fray, and those two men somehow persuaded a small boy to release them. Instead of going straight back to camp, they sought out the village head-man, who, to save his own skin, had stopped at home, and bore him off a prisoner to Colonel Bower. A man in No. 4 had his father killed in the attack on Captain Watson's camp, which would have been sufficient reason for him to have decided that our service was no place for him, but he remained firm. There were a great number of similar instances of loyalty in every company, but, when we consider the remarkable loyalty of the men as a whole, it is quite unnecessary to give any more instances of individuals. The regiment, as will be seen, bore their

part with the best, in the strife a few weeks
later, but it is certain that their behaviour against
their own folk about Wei-hai-wei is something to
be very proud of. It proved, beyond a doubt that
they were thoroughly to be relied on.

The newspapers were full of it all at the time,
and Sir Claude Macdonald, the British Minister at
Peking, wired to the Commissioner :—" Please congratulate Colonel Bower on the splendid behaviour
of his regiment."

Although all had now sunk into its normal state
of rural peace, and the farmers, who, not long
before, had thirsted for our blood now desired
only our hard-earned dollars, had returned to their
homes and their work on the fields, it was still considered advisable to make some display of force in
the affected regions, and so three camps were formed
round the boundary, in addition to the supply camp
already referred to, and the regiment remained out
for about a month, until the middle of June. The
Boundary Commission returned to Wei-hai-wei on
the 18th of May.

At this time the troubles farther north were beginning to materialise, although out in camp we
heard but little of it all, except that ships were
constantly leaving the harbour for Taku, and that
every available Marine from the island and main-
land had been ordered north.

On the 11th June most of the companies returned
to Matou from the boundary, one camp and the
supply camp remaining out until the 18th.

It was on this latter date that we began to hear
the war trumpets sound in real earnest. No. 4
Company, made up to 100 strong, under Captain
Watson, with Lieutenants Bray and Ollivant, and
Colour-Sergeant Purdon, was warned for service,
and was, in fact, on the lighters for conveyance
to H.M.S. *Peacock,* which was to take it to
Taku, when the *Endymion* arrived to cancel the
move, and the men were reluctantly landed again.
It is as well that this was so, for it is an established
fact that the Chinese are far better under their own
officers, and, therefore, the mixing and " making up "
of companies, so dear to the older-fashioned staff
officer, are a great mistake when applied to the
Chinese regiment.   It is only natural that men
are going to follow the man who has struggled
to teach them to be soldiers for some time, far
better and more readily than the comparative
stranger, whom they have only seen drilling other
men afar off.   Things were, however, coming
our way all the same, for, two days later, on
the 20th June, the destroyer *Whiting* arrived
from Taku, with a shell in her boiler, to say that
H.M.S. *Orlando* was on its way to take us, or rather
200 of us, to the front, and that that number was

to be ready to embark as soon as she arrived. This party was made up as under :—

> Lieut.-Colonel H. Bower in command, with Capt. Montgomerie as Adjutant.
>
> No. 2 Coy.—Capt. Barnes, Lieut. Layard, and Col.-Sergt. Dunn.
>
> No. 4 Coy.—Capt. Watson, Lieut. Bray, and Col.-Sergt. Purdon.
>
> No. 5 Coy.—Capt. Hill and Lieut. Fairfax.
>
> No. 6 Coy.—Capt. Menzies, Lieut. Ollivant, and Col.-Sergt. Whittaker.

Each company of the above finding fifty men, more or less, according to their effective strength of trained men.

The party reached the *Orlando* at 8 P.M., and left at 5 A.M. next day. There was also on board a small party of the Royal Engineers, who did yeoman's work in Tientsin later on, under Captain Lee, R.E.

PART II

THE FIGHTING ROUND TIENTSIN

CHAPTER IV

IT is often very hard to induce people, especially if they belong to the Indian contingent, which, unfortunately, arrived after all the real stiff fighting was over, to believe that there was any fighting worth talking about in and about Tientsin, and harder still to get into their heads that the 1st Chinese Regiment took any part therein. Still, a glance at the contemporary prints of that time will serve to prove, to the most unbelieving, that both these statements are based on a solid foundation of fact.

It is doubly unfortunate that the splendid contingent that arrived subsequently from India was not at Tientsin in the earlier days of the troubles of that sorely-tried port, because it would have given to Great Britain that right to speak with decision, and to act, if need be, with independence, which the smallness of our force denied to our country. We were able to bear our share of all that came along, but independent action was never

Men of the 1st Chinese Regiment in Field Service Order.

possible, as it was, to a certain extent, after the troops from India arrived at Tientsin.

Let us now turn from conjecture to fact, and follow the fortunes of the first party to leave Wei-hai-wei, whose departure on board H.M.S. *Orlando* has already been mentioned.   Taku anchorage was reached at 5 A.M., on the 22nd June, after a somewhat uneventful voyage, which was occupied to a certain extent by the officers in cutting one another's hair, a luxury the conveniences of camp life on the boundary did not run to, with varying success.   During the short stay of the *Orlando* at Chefoo, the Japanese flagship arrived, and was received with the customary salute, the guard and bugler being found by the regiment, as all the Marines had been landed.

As soon as we arrived, preparations were made to land us, and the destroyer *Fame* came alongside for that purpose, and we began to load men, rations, and ammunition into her, and into one of the *Orlando's* barges.   By 8 A.M. all was ready, and we cast off.   As things were a bit late, and the tide was beginning to fall on the bar, we started at the best speed compatible with the safety of the barge, towing astern, for Tongku.   We had not gone far, however, when the men in the barge began to make signals of distress, so that our speed was very much reduced.   However, when we had got to the lightship, the barge was palpably sinking. It was, accordingly, brought alongside and emptied, the ammunition being added to the things on the *Fame's* already crowded deck, and the bags of flour and rice being cast into the sea. However, we eventually arrived all correct somewhere about noon. As we were tying up at Tongku, we had our first experience of the actual horrors of war, in the form of three unfortunate Chinese trying to escape from the Russians by swimming across the Peiho. Their efforts were in vain, for they were all shot in the water close to the farther bank.

After some delay, owing to the difficulty of providing us with a train, we started, with a party from H.M.S. *Terrible*, for the end of the railway, near Chang-lien-cheng, about 4 P.M. There were a few civilians, mostly connected with the railway and the shipping, to see us off, and they promised us a hot time on the way; but, beyond a few scattered horsemen, who viewed us from afar off, we saw no signs of any troops, bar a few of the Allies, scattered along the line. Our train proceeded with a caution that spoke volumes for the care for our safety on the part of the engineer, and we finally arrived at the Railhead at 11 P.M., having gone fourteen miles since 4 P.M. The country on both sides of the line, and all about Railhead, was quite deserted, and the whole horizon was blotted with the smoke of burning hamlets. The Russians got the credit for this destruction, but no one can say whether they were maligned or not. It was a most curious thing, and one that was always noticeable during the advance of the Allies, both on Tientsin and on Peking, how completely the country people managed to disappear on these occasions, and one could not but wonder where they all got to, as that part of the country is, as a rule, most densely populated. Many of the people living between Taku and Tientsin took refuge in junks and sampans on the Peiho, but it is a mystery where the huge remainder went.

We got to work as soon as it was light, to unload the train, which had to go back to Tongku to bring up other troops, and when we were beginning, could see the party of the Royal Welsh Fusiliers and the Naval Brigade starting for Tientsin. Of course, there was no help for it, so we had to remain behind to guard the large quantity of ammunition we had brought up, as there was absolutely no transport of any kind to take it forward. The day was spent under more or less warlike conditions, with sentries and groups placed at the various defensible points. There were one or two alarms, fifteen hundred Chinese cavalry, amongst other items, being at one time reported to the south-west, who, however, gave us a wide berth. In point of fact, the majority of us never saw the shadow of an enemy, except one prisoner who made good his escape from the Naval guard, and caused a diversion by the number of shots fired after him to persuade him either to stop or return —in vain. Towards evening we heard, with great thankfulness, that Tientsin had been relieved.

The next morning the detachment of the Hong-Kong regiment arrived, and at noon two of their companies, with our Nos. 2 and 4 Companies, the whole under Colonel Bower, started for Tientsin, escorting a naval 12-pounder gun and its ammunition. Escorting guns very soon means dragging them, as we have often found out, and it was so in this case. No. 2 Company, as rearguard, had its hands quite full with the three carts of ammunition and odds and ends, and No. 4 had to take turns with the four half-companies of the Hong-Kong regiment at pulling the gun. It was a most trying march, and only those who were present can have any idea of the grand work our men put in. The men of the Hong-Kong regiment, having been some days on board ship, were in poor condition, and their spells became shorter and shorter as the day went on. With the best will in the world, and the most willing spirit, their flesh was weak, and finally the task of dragging that 12-pounder into Tientsin

fell entirely on No. 4 Company, which task, to
their eternal honour be it recorded, they right
manfully accomplished.

We passed through many deserted villages on
the way, deserted, that is, by the human inhabitants only, for there were dogs there, and poultry
—some of which came along lost in wonder, to all
appearances, as to the departure of their masters.
Many, too, were the awesome sights we saw along
the river banks, whenever we struck it, and some
of them made us cease from wondering at the sleek
and contented looks of the village dogs, usually so
thin and starved.   At one time, in the afternoon,
a bend in the river brought us suddenly in full
view of the tug *Fa-wan* feeling its way cautiously
downstream to Taku.   Our appearance, where
no troops were expected, seemed to cause them
some excitement, for they stopped and cleared for
action, so far as a mere tug can perform this com-
plicated evolution.   However, we met, and then
parted, both as friends.

Arriving at the outskirts of Tientsin Settlement
about 5 P.M., we came upon the Russians shelling
the Peiyang, or Eastern Arsenal, but without much
apparent effect.   As we skirted their camp, much
interest was displayed by both parties, but they
carefully abstained from rendering us any assistance
in dragging our gun and carts up the steep, sandy

track from the plain, on which they were in camp, to the railway line passing through the Mud Wall, which seemed to be our only means of entrance into the Settlement. The task was eventually accomplished without their assistance, and the way No. 4 got the gun up the railway embankment was one of the grandest sights of the day.

By this time it was growing dark, and No. 2 Company, following the only apparent road, passed through several villages burnt to the ground, and eventually arrived on the enemy's side of the railway station, the officer in command being brought up short by a Russian sentry drawing a bead on him. Fortunately, the Chinese were not then paying such a close attention to the railway station as they did subsequently, or things would not have been so peaceably arranged. It was now quite apparent, in the waning light, that the carts were on the wrong side of the line to be quite safe, so Captain Barnes climbed up the nearest signal-post to reconnoitre, fortunately for him, escaping the attention of any snipers. It being necessary to get the carts over the six or eight pairs of rails running through the station as soon as could be, and, as the Russians confined their "assisting" to the French interpretation of the word, there was no help for it but No. 2 must do the job unaided. And do it they did, in the grandest way. Carts, rats of ponies, and all, were lifted bodily over the highest of the rails, and dragged over the others. A large party of coolies, piloted by Captain Burke, R.N., now arrived, and relieved us of our charges.

As we marched through the French Concession, almost entirely in ruins, we became aware, for the first time, of the presence of snipers. I do not think there is anything less agreeable than the ordinary sniper; but when you hear him for the first time at night, when his bullet goes "ping-pinging" amongst telegraph lines and corrugated iron buildings, he really has something of a romantic touch about him. On our march through the streets we were received with a large amount of applause at various points, for, I fancy, the inhabitants had not quite got over their joy at their first relief, and were glad to welcome any reinforcements, even though they belonged to the race that had proved so bitterly hostile. The feeling against the Chinese race as a whole was so great, as a matter of fact, in Tientsin, that the good folk there did not appreciate us a bit, and we even heard that there were some who were opposed to our entry into their sacred Settlement at all, though this does not sound likely considering the danger the place was in. There is little doubt, however, that much of the totally false and unnecessary reports about the regiment emanated from the fertile brains

of residents of the place, whose time during the
siege was spent mostly in cellars, for it is certain
that no one who was on the earth, and saw our
men in action, could have fathered some of the
lies that have since been written and spoken about
the Chinese regiment.

CHAPTER V

THAT night, and for the next few days, No. 2 was accommodated in a godown next the Welsh Fusiliers and men of the *Barfleur*, while No. 4 were put up in a similar store on the Bund, the two having got separated somehow in the march through the French Settlement. The officers put up in a house in Victoria Terrace.

Next day, the 25th, No. 2 went on piquet duty at the Recreation Ground and Woollen Mills, with a company of the Hong-Kong regiment, but nothing exciting happened that night. The following day, owing to the number of snipers who were gradually closing in on the defences through the villages and ruins to the west of the Recreation Ground, three sections of No. 2 and one half of the company of the Hong-Kong regiment moved out in the afternoon to drive them back, and to destroy one or two small huts which seemed to have a great attraction for an inordinate number of men, who, being armed, could not have been peacefully inclined. Quite a little battle was the result, though no harm was done to our side, and not a great deal to the enemy. It was just like stirring up a hornet's nest, for Chinese, Boxers, and troops seemed to crop up everywhere, and fire anywhere. This was especially the case on the right of our line of advance, where the French outposts on the Taku Road were not far from the native city, and the troops lining it and the salt heaps on their side of the river.   There, apparently, the Chinese thought the French were leading a grand attack against them, and *vice versa,* for both parties got to work with a will, and a noise like Pandemonium was the result.   Meantime, the party which had caused all this commotion quietly withdrew, having effected its purpose in discouraging the snipers for a day or two.   Though the fire on them was but ill-aimed, it was our men's baptism of fire, so to say, under which they showed the greatest steadiness.

This 26th June was a great day in Tientsin, for on it Admiral Seymour's brave men returned from their unsuccessful attempt to reach Peking. The regiment had no hand in his relief at Hsiku Arsenal, for, although we were warned to fall in for this service at 11.30 P.M. on the 24th, as we only marched in to the Settlement at 9.30 P.M., the authorities thought it would be trying the men a bit high, after the great labours they had gone through that day.

On the evening of the 26th, Colonel Dorward,

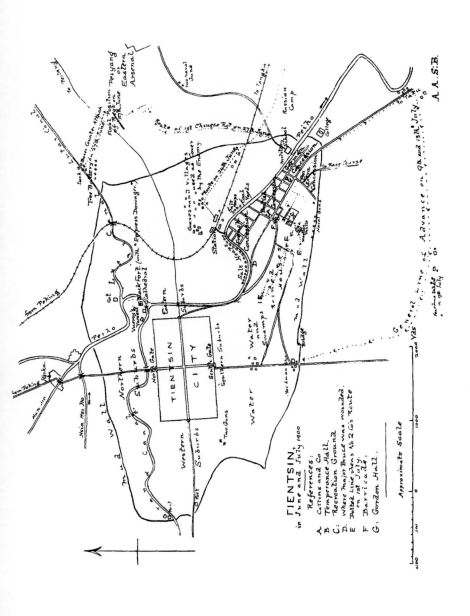

TIENTSIN,
in June and July 1900

References:

A. Collins and Co.
B. Temperance Hall.
C. Recreation Ground.
D. Where Major Bruce was wounded.
E. Dotted line shens No 2 Co's Route on 1st July.
F. Barricade.
G. Gordon Hall.

Approximate Scale

A.A.S.B.

our Civil and Military Commissioner, who had been appointed to command the troops in North China, with the rank of Brigadier-General, arrived with our No. 5 Company, under Captain Hill. At the same time also arrived the Hong-Kong and Singapore Artillery, under Major St John, with which gallant band we were afterwards so closely connected on more than one occasion. We were very glad to see all these troops, few as they were, as they all helped to give us a vote.

The 27th June will always be remembered by us as the first time the regiment, more or less, was on the field of battle. On that particular morning the Russians, whose camp was close to it, started out to take the big Eastern or Peiyang Arsenal, somewhat to the dismay of some of the residents of Tientsin, who averred that there were enough explosives stored there to destroy the whole of the Settlement and city if they were let off. Two of us watched the attack from the top of the Gordon Hall tower, and about 10 A.M. could see that the Russians were being decidedly worsted, for part of their line was retiring at no mean speed, while the rest was halted. The Chinese in the Arsenal, especially at its northern end, seemed to have got the range of a small hut in the plain in front of them, for every time any of the Russians got near it a heavy fire,

c

whose bullets we could see kicking up the ground
all about the hut, broke out. It struck us, on
our tower, that reinforcements would soon be in
demand, and, sure enough, from all sides came
heated people seeking General Dorward, Colonel
Bower, and other officers.

So we all fell in, and, by great good luck, the
details of which need not be specified, we found
ourselves—that is, Colonel Bower and his adjutant,
Captain Montgomerie, No. 2 Company, with Captain
Barnes, Lieutenant Layard, and Colour-Sergeant
Dunn, No. 4 Company, with Captain Watson, Lieutenant Bray, and Colour-Sergeant Purdon, and
No. 5 Company, with Captains Hill and Fairfax—on
the plain midway between the Settlement and the
Arsenal, advancing over the very ground where we
had, an hour before, seen the Russians retire, in
extended order, with the Naval Brigade, who had
gone out a good time before us, away to our front
and quite close to the enemy's position.

Very soon we could hear their cheers as they
rushed the place, and so, a further advance
seeming needless, the Colonel halted us. We had
only been halted a few minutes when, away on
our left, by the Lutai Canal, we saw a horde of
troops and Boxers pouring over the plain in the
direction of the Arsenal, with the evident intention of taking our force there in rear. We

at once changed our front so as to face this new
development, and advanced, in the hopes of
coming, at any rate, within close range. Owing
to the absence of rain the plain where we were
was a regular khaki colour, which rendered us
quite invisible to the enemy, and we were all
convinced that had not a Russian company come
up on either flank of us in their white
coats and black trousers, and opened fire as
well, we should have had a pretty fight. As
it was, our fire had already had some considerable effect on the enemy, the more so
as they had not the least idea whence it came, and
they seemed not at all sure what to do; for some
went on, others went back, and the rest stood still
and waved their flags. However, the advent of the
Russians gave the show away, and, for a time, we
came under a certain amount of fire, mostly over our
heads, for, beyond one man having a hole bored in
the slack of his trousers, and another one in the
heel of his boot, I heard of no casualties. Before
we had become regularly engaged, we had seen,
between us and the enemy, a dark figure approaching us, waving his arms in such a way as to give
rise to the idea that he was a Boxer leader, and he
was nearly fired at for that reason. It was, however,
soon seen that he was a Marine, severely wounded
in both legs, escaping from the enemy. It appeared

that he and another had been wounded during the advance of the Marines over that part of the field, and had been left for the stretcher party to bring in. The Chinese got there first, however, and our friend was lucky enough to get away and escape the fate of his comrade, who was killed and decapitated. The Chinese having retired whence they came out, the troops all returned from the Arsenal, which was handed over to the Russians. We waited on the field for some little time longer, covering the operations of a search party, who went out to look for the other Marine I have referred to.

No account of this battle would be complete without mentioning our old pal the 12-pounder, which was posted near the gap in the Mud Wall through which No. 4 Company had pulled it on the 24th. It did great work, and about 11 A.M., when we were on our way out, put a shell into a large magazine in the Arsenal. The explosion that followed was one of the most lovely, and, at the same time, the most extraordinary, sights I have ever seen. A huge pillar of snowy whiteness rose slowly and majestically into the air, and when its summit was five or six hundred feet above the earth, it slowly opened out like a vast sunshade, and after hanging in the air for ten minutes or so, slowly dissolved. I have since seen summer clouds of similar appearance, but never anything to surpass this death-dealing cloud

for the beauty of its pure whiteness. It was soon
followed by two lesser ones, which must have done
a lot of damage among them.

Our men behaved like old soldiers on this day,
taking not the least notice of the bullets whistling
over them. The section commanders also maintained a perfect control over their men, and the
section volley-firing was very good, the objects being
clearly pointed out. It was very lucky for us that
the enemy brought out so many flags of so many
different colours and shapes, as these helped our
native non - commissioned officers wonderfully in
their selection of the object to aim at. We really
felt that they deserved our thanks, only that they
would not stay to receive them.

We were lucky enough to be mentioned in
General Dorward's despatch home by wire, as having
"repulsed a flank attack of Boxers, inflicting considerable loss on the enemy," which we certainly
did. Eye-witnesses on the Gordon Hall tower, who
were unable to see us on that khaki ground except
when we advanced, said that our fire knocked out
quite a number, an advantage of which the flatness
of the plain and a queer mirage, that troubled us at
times, deprived us ourselves.

On the 28th a big fire broke out in some large
stores towards the German Concession, and No. 2
Company was sent off at the double to try and

get it under. The appliances were, however, too
limited and the fire had too good a hold for their
efforts to be of much avail, so they were ordered to
procure a quantity of flour and other food stuffs out
of some bakers' shops near by, which were subsequently destroyed by the same fire, palpably the
work of incendiaries. Quite a lot of valuable stuff
was saved and sent in carts to the Gordon Hall, for
the use of the women and children. I mention this
little incident (at which our men worked very hard
and successfully), because the regiment got the
credit of having set the place on fire in the first
instance—one of the uncharitable things said, and
readily believed by some, about our men. When
we heard the story we were all more amazed at
the nerve of those who started it, than anything
else, as it was our first experience of that sort of
mischief.

The remainder of the men were mostly employed
on fatigue unloading junks which the naval
authorities had collected to bring up stores, etc.,
from Taku, and which were full of salt and such
like.

The men moved into Collins & Co.'s godowns
on the Consular Road, and the officers mostly into
the Temperance Hall, on the corner of the Taku
road. General Dorward and his staff also took up
their quarters in the same building, and continued

to mess with us.   The Hong-Kong gunners and the officers of the Hong-Kong regiment were also in the building, the General's idea being to get us all together near that portion of the defences allotted to his command, the Welsh Fusiliers being a little farther east along the Taku road.

This fatigue work continued for the next two days, unloading junks being alternated with collecting coal across the river and bringing it over, not a pleasant job, owing to the number of corpses in the water, and to the fact that the coal-yard was much favoured by snipers.   No. 4 Company was sent down the river on the 30th to Railhead Camp to help at loading stores on lighters, returning on the 3rd of July.

CHAPTER VI

THE closing in of the snipers once more among the ruins west of the Recreation Ground gave rise to the idea that the enemy were pushing their investing lines too close in that direction. A mixed force, under Colonel Bower, was therefore sent out on the 1st July to see what was going on, and to drive back the bold, bad men. This force consisted of two 2.5-inch guns of the Hong-Kong Artillery, and the following, given in the order in which they subsequently advanced, taken from right (the Taku road side) to left : 50 Japanese Infantry, No. 2 Company, 50 men of the Hong-Kong regiment, and 50 American Marines, with 100 of the Welsh Fusiliers as a general reserve. We were extended in the above order from the Taku road to the Mud Wall, and advanced, clearing the houses of the desperadoes there, who scuttled off like rabbits, not a few being brought down. We went on like this for, possibly, 500 yards, when we were brought up against a regular little fort, which consisted of four parallel rows of well-built brick houses, with the openings at each end barricaded so as to form one square work. This was stormed in great style by

40

Lieutenant Layard, at the head of his half-company, he bayoneting two men in the assault. The other half-company, under Colour-Sergeant Dunn, remained on one flank, covering the assault, and giving the enemy a hot fire as they retired.

While this was going on I was more or less between the two half-companies, attended by the faithful Liu, my interpreter, and my bugler, Li ping chen, both lads of under eighteen. We apparently attracted the attention of a man about 300 yards off, armed with a large bore weapon of sorts, which fired evil-sounding slugs, with smoky powder. We could see the smoke of his gun, then hear the report, and presently the missile came "bizz-bizz-bizzing" towards us. He was no mean marksman, for all his old-fashioned gun, for he sent half-a-dozen shots very adjacent to us, one in particular passing between Liu and me. I said to him: "This does not seem to be a very good place we have selected," but he merely answered: "No, sir," with a smile, being quite unmoved by the danger. The bugler, on his part, was trying to pick off our friend. I mention this incident merely as an instance of the cold-blooded courage of our men.

We now proceeded to set this abode of snipers on fire, as it was full of ammunition we could not possibly remove, and which rattled right merrily when the place was well alight. The "Retire" now sounded with a frequency that betokened some urgency, so Lieutenant Layard drew off his half-company, under cover of the fire of that of Colour-Sergeant Dunn, into the shelter of a row of houses in ruins, that had formed the side of a road at right angles to our line of advance, I remaining behind at the opening to cover, in turn, with six men, the retirement of the Colour-Sergeant's lot. By this time things were getting very lively, for the Chinese had re-occupied the unburnt part of their fort and the adjacent houses, and were pouring in a hot fire on us from a very close range. It was then that I saw one of the most daring things it has ever been my lot to witness. The Colour-Sergeant's men were in and among a lot of grave mounds about fifty yards to my front, when suddenly on one of the mounds there upstood one of the men, Wang kwo hsing by name, loading and firing as coolly as if on the range, whenever he saw a chance. How he escaped being shot through and through is a marvel, but he did. In fact, strange as it may seem, we had not a man hit, a bit of luck that I ascribe entirely to the closeness of the enemy. This may seem a little too tall, but it is a well-known fact that in most of the fighting at that time the men in the firing line were never hit, while those in the reserves, and beyond, lost most; and rifles picked up on the field were always found with the back-sights as high as they would go. I am, personally, of opinion that these Boxers fancied that the higher you put the sight the harder the bullet went, and so, with the amiable intention of doing us the maximum amount of injury, always kept them at the top.

It appears that the party of the Hong-Kong regiment, which was on our left and left rear, found itself hard pressed, and the officer in command sent two messages to this effect to Colonel Bower, who, thereupon, sent back to the General for assistance, his whole force being by this time engaged all along the line, in case the enemy, emboldened by our retirement, should follow us in such force as to threaten the Settlement, for there were lots of them there by this time. Accordingly, other troops were hurried out, but Colonel Bower's party had been withdrawn and the Chinese showed no signs of coming on. Among the troops that turned out to rescue us was No. 7 Company, which, with Major Bruce, Captain Pereira, Lieutenant Brooke, and Colour-Sergeant Brook had just arrived from Wei-hai-wei, and which, with No. 5, extended outside the defences to cover our retirement.

On this occasion, in one of the hardest tests

that a soldier can be put to—namely, retiring under fire—the men, one and all, showed the most perfect courage, moving as steadily as though they were on the hills round the barracks at Matou. There was no sign of haste to get away, and never the least confusion, the orders being obeyed with absolute discipline. Far from showing any desire to retire (the boot was on the other leg rather), they did not at all see that it was necessary to retire, and would have preferred to stay where they were, and make the Boxers go. The Hong-Kong regiment had two killed and three wounded.

CHAPTER VII

FOR the next day or two we were kept pretty hard at work on fatigues of various sorts, among them being the strengthening of our part of the defences by means of a line of trenches connecting the Mud Wall with the Taku road. This line was never actually finished, as Tientsin city was taken before this could be done, for our force was so small that it was very hard to find men for the various duties, and fatigues naturally came after them.

About this time an order was issued that one-half of each unit was to sleep with equipment on, all ready to turn out at a moment's notice. This was a good thing, for on the 2nd there were two very determined attacks on the railway station at night, in consequence of which everyone was turned out twice, and most of them only succeeded in getting in one another's way, as is so apt to be the case when a lot of people turn out suddenly in the dark and the rain, and all want to do something, or to know something.

It must be clearly understood that all this time we were being subjected to a shell fire from the

45

city and forts round it, which increased very much
in severity as time went on and the enemy got
up more guns from Lutai and other places. For
some reason these attentions were not responded
to until the 6th July, although we had eleven guns
of sorts. At the time we used to hear that our
abstinence from what seemed to the ordinary run
of us only our just dues, was at the request of the
merchants of Tientsin, who realised the vast losses
that would accrue to them if much damage was
done, and this story may or may not be true.
Any way, we were all delighted when we heard,
on the morning of the 6th aforesaid, that the native
city was to be shelled that afternoon, for our guns
had hitherto confined their attentions to the Hai-
kwan-ssu, or Western Arsenal, and to any stray
bodies who appeared outside the city. At 2 P.M.,
accordingly, the first bombardment of the city
began, the following guns taking part : naval guns,
two 12-pounders, two 9-pounders, and one 6-
pounder ; two Krupp guns captured at the Taku
Forts, and worked by men of the Royal Marines ;
four 2.5-inch muzzle-loading, smoky powder-guns
of the Hong-Kong Artillery, and a Japanese mountain battery of smoky powder pop-guns, very handy
to move about, but of medium range only. This
formidable battery, then, began the attempt to
reduce Tientsin to civility, those guns that could

carry as far being directed at the Viceroy's Yamen, and the fort near it, while the others were content with the pagodas and things on and near the city walls. The immediate effect of this fire was to make the enemy leave off, although only for a time.

I must, however, not run on too fast, but must take things as they came along. On the 3rd July we were treated to a very heavy shell fire, which was directed mainly at the house where Admiral Seymour was, and at the Temperance Hall, where General Dorward and all of us lived. A small shell burst in the room next to mine, which was occupied by three officers of the regiment. Fortunately, no one was in it at the time, for it made most awful havoc, and would have knocked a man to pieces, had there been one there.

We began the 4th of July at digging more trenches, but in the afternoon various signs of an impending attack of some size made us exchange the shovel for the rifle. It is safe to say that on this occasion the Settlement was attacked with vigour, from that part of the Mud Wall where the naval guns were to the railway station, the attack being everywhere repulsed. We were ordered down to the station to reinforce the garrison there, which was being rather roughly handled. On the same errand went a number of bluejackets, who arrived a little before us. We doubled through the French Concession, up one road and down another, with the bullets, which were all coming over the station, whistling their vicious note over our heads as we ran. To add to these pleasantries, it began to rain in torrents, so thick, in fact, that we could only see a short way in front. At most of the corners as we went along, we came upon small parties of French Marines from Tonkin, who had evidently stopped to rest awhile on their way to reinforce their comrades at the station, some of whom would rise up and come on with us. My company being in front, I had hard work to keep the Colonel, who was leading, in sight, as well as an eye on my men to see that they did not take a wrong turning, as few of them knew more about the place than I did. Eventually we reached the station, and here the din was appalling. Rifles incessantly crackling all round, bullets pattering on the corrugated iron or singing away over the Settlement, and a perfect deluge of rain falling impartially on the lot, made a combination of noise that was bewildering, to say the least of it. Some of the leading companies formed up behind a brick wall, with a number of officers and men of the *Centurion*, while the rest lay down behind and under some trucks in rear of the station

The Post-Office corner at Tientsin during the siege.

buildings. The infantry attack had now been beaten off, and, beyond their still heavy fire, we could see no trace of the enemy. They were not, however, going to let us down so easily, for as soon as their foot-men had drawn off, and knowing full well that the station buildings were full of troops, they started a very hot shell fire on them and on the Bridge-of-Boats over the Peiho, from no less than eleven guns, five of which at what was called the Tree Battery, being not more than 1800 or 2000 yards away to the north-east. Having the range of the station to a yard, they pitched shell after shell all about us, with an occasional shrapnel over the bridge. They put ten shots, in rapid succession, round the naval maxim and knocked it out, which, as it was firing black powder, is not to be wondered at. We had an example of the surprising lack of effect that attends even the best aimed shell fire, as this was; for, during it all, we had only one man hit, Bugler Li ping chen, who was hit in the thigh by a fragment of a shell. The other parties had a certain amount of casualties, but, as far as one could see, they were mostly from rifle fire. It was a merciful thing that a shell did not strike that thin brick wall, for behind it were men, bluejackets and our men, in some places five or six deep. The behaviour of our

D

men under these most trying conditions was
perfect, and, far from being "shaken" by the fire,
they seemed to regard it with indifference.   I
saw one shell burst in some lime only a few feet
from the left of No. 4 Company, which was lying
down behind the row of trucks.   It covered the
men about there with lime, which they appeared to
look on as an immense joke, judging from the shouts
of laughter which arose from them.   After an hour
and a half of this, we received orders to return
to the Settlement, which we were not loth to
do, being wet to the skin.   The enemy seemed
to get wind of our move as soon as we did, for
they burst a number of shell over the bridge,
one of which took off a large portion of the fore-
arm of a man of No. 2, just on the border of
the French Concession.   The poor chap afterwards
died.   Another man of No. 7 was shot through
the leg, whilst crossing the bridge, by an ever-ready
sniper.   It will be seen that this day, though
without any very tangible results, let us see our
men under shell fire, and I am sure none of us
were disappointed at their behaviour under the
trying conditions of being unable to make any
reply at all, effective or otherwise.

The following morning General Dorward, accompanied by Colonel Bower and Major Bruce, visited
the station and its environs on a tour of inspection,

being escorted by No. 2 Company. While they were out to the front looking over the ground, we were left behind another wall not much thicker than our friend of the previous day, as the enemy's shell-fire was being continued unabated. Beyond showing a wise and natural preference for the thicker parts of the wall, the men seemed to regard the fire with the same indifference as before, except that, the day being fine, they were more cheerful.

That same evening thirty men of the same company escorted the Admiral on a similar errand, being in charge of Lieutenant Layard. Beyond these little expeditions, and the usual shelling, there was no incident of any particular moment that day as far as we were concerned; but the enemy placed two large guns in the Hai-kwan-ssu Arsenal, with which they enfiladed our naval guns on the Mud Wall, and a brisk duel ensued, the Chinese after an hour or so retiring.

I have already referred to the bombardment of the city on the 6th, and, beyond mentioning that three Marines were injured by a premature burst of a shell fired from one of the captured Krupps, I need say no more about that part of the day's proceedings.

We were very heavily shelled, and no less than six different sorts of shells struck the Temperance Hall, where the General and the rest of us lived, in about ten minutes, clearly proving that the Chinese spies had given us away. Two shells, fortunately both " blind," passed through the table where the Royal Artillery officers were at lunch, without hurting anyone. They ceased lunching. A shrapnel burst in the main entrance hall, making a great mess, but hurting no one. The next was not so kind, for, passing through in the same flight, it burst in the yard behind, and wounded Lieutenant Browne, R.E., who was passing, in three or four places, one in the sole of his foot being the most troublesome. A big yellow bath, which was also in the way, presented a curious sight when the bullets had done with it, being more like a sieve than its own more useful self.

Two of us had gone up to the Gordon Hall tower to see the fun, and found there a Frenchman and a Russian with the same object. We were enjoying the view, when a shell from the " Empress Dowager," as the big gun near the Yamen was affectionately termed, came screeching over our heads at no great distance and burst in the Victoria Road, about a hundred yards behind. One of our foreign friends remembered a very pressing engagement below, and the other, after a second shell, had a similar recollection. A third, in the same place, made us glad enough to get out too, and, as we were descending, a fourth struck the German Club to our right front.

CHAPTER VIII

ABOUT noon, on this same day, a mixed force, consisting of Nos. 2, 5, and 7 Companies, four officers and 100 men of the Royal Navy, and two officers and 100 men of the American Marine Corps, the whole under the command of Major Bruce, made a reconnaissance westwards along the Taku road, through the French Concession towards the river. The object of the movement was to locate, and silence, if possible, one or two Chinese guns which had taken up a position in that direction, and were causing us no little annoyance. Soon after passing the last French barricade the advance party, with whom was Major Bruce, became engaged, and pushing on up to where the road debouches on to the river, took up a position to cover the advance of the remainder of the force. Parties, both of our men and of bluejackets, continued the advance under a heavy fire from the salt heaps across the river, beyond the open river bank to some ruined houses farther along. From this spot the enemy's gun could be clearly seen, and was found, unfortunately, to be on a spit of land across the river. A brisk fire from each side went on for some time;

53

but, as the gun could not be damaged without
artillery, our troops were gradually withdrawn, a
movement which was carried out with steadiness.

In the afternoon Major Bruce, having been given
a naval 9-pounder gun, decided to renew the
attempt, accompanied by a somewhat smaller force
of infantry. It became apparent, shortly after
passing the French lines, that the enemy had made
additional preparations to dispute these attentions.
The advance party, under Captain Fairfax, was
again exposed to a heavy fire, which was much
more concentrated, sweeping down the only road
by which the gun could be brought up. Nevertheless, the force pushed on, taking advantage of what
little cover was afforded by the ruined and burnt-
out mud walls on either side of the road, until the
open space by the river bank was again reached.
Here the order was given for the gun to come
into action, Captains Hill, Fairfax, and Lieutenant
Brooke, with some men of the regiment, covering
the movement with their fire from a low parapet
along the river bank. Twice the gun's crew
endeavoured to come into action, and both times
were they driven back by the intensity of the
heavy fire poured in upon them at close range. In
addition to rifle fire, the enemy were also bursting
shrapnel all round the party, and the fire became
so murderous that there was no alternative but to

withdraw the gun. This proved to be a very hard task. The enemy had by this time come much closer, and as soon as the gun's crew attempted to hook on the drag-ropes and turn the gun, they were met by such a concentrated fire that they were driven back. However, you can trust the British sailor to do what he starts out to do, and, in spite of the heavy fire, the gun was eventually got under cover and withdrawn. The solid pluck required to face that fire in a great clump is only typical of the British " Blue."

The troops had now drawn off, except five or six of our men, who, with Major Bruce, Captain Hill, and Lieutenant Brooke, remained to cover the retirement to the end. Owing to the nature of the ground, which was covered with a mass of burnt-out ruins, communication was very hard, and some of the advance party, under Captain Fairfax, became detached, but were soon found by Major Bruce and Captain Hill, who at once went in search of them. As they were rejoining the rest, Captain Hill had a very narrow escape. A shell burst, seemingly, just over his head. One of our men, who was nearly touching him, was killed, and another badly hit. Almost immediately after this, as the retirement continued, Major Bruce received a bullet through his helmet, and then one through his body, it passing through his liver. The retirement was concluded in good order, the Chinese following it up almost to the French barricade.

Our men behaved exceedingly well under the most trying ordeal to which they were exposed.

The losses sustained on this occasion were very heavy.   As we have seen, Major Bruce was severely wounded, while two of our men were killed and five wounded.   The Naval Brigade also suffered severely, Midshipman F. Esdaile, of H.M.S. *Barfleur*, being mortally wounded, and four men, more or less severely.

CHAPTER IX

It will excite no wonder in anyone's mind to be told that the next day, the 7th July, we all left the Temperance Hall for more retired quarters. The officers of the regiment went partly into the house of a Mr Emens, on Consular Road, and partly into the house of Mr W. W. Dickinson, of Collins & Co., whose house adjoined the godowns of that firm in which our men were already quartered. It is hard at this distance of time to appreciate the change it was for us, from the mere empty squalor of our previous surroundings to the luxury of our new abode. In the former our comforts had been non-existent, for we had nothing but the hasty campaign kit we had arrived with; our food had been of the least inviting: cold bully beef for breakfast, stewed ditto for lunch, and curried ditto for dinner, having been the daily menu, shared, as I have said, by the General and his staff. Now we rejoiced in all the comforts of a home, chairs, tables, table-linen, and, best of all, a good cook and a consequent variety of food. The General moved into the house of Mr Cousens, of Jardine, Matheson & Co.

The shelling of the city was continued, and the

57

enemy replied with some success. One shell entered the barracks of the men of the *Centurion*, killing two and wounding three. In the afternoon the enemy broke out in a new place, by opening fire from four guns to the south-west of our guns on the Mud Wall, which were thus under fire from no less than three sides. These guns were afterwards captured, as will be seen, on the 9th July.

Captain Dent, Lieutenants Toke and Johnson, with Nos. 1 and 3, the remaining companies of the regiment, arrived this day from Wei-hai-wei.

We had, that evening, an example of the excellence of the Chinese Intelligence Department. The house of Mr Dickinson had not, up to date, been hit at all; but that evening, when we were at dinner, a shell burst in the verandah of the dining-room. It luckily did little harm, though a segment of it grazed the top of my head. Shortly after, another came into the bathroom of the room above the dining-room, but did not burst. I am convinced they both came from our friends we had essayed to silence the day before. About the same time, Mr Cousens, into whose house General Dorward had moved, was hit in the leg by a sniper, while he was in bed. The sniper, as many were, was said to be in the Settlement. In fact, the whole place was said to be full of spies, who alternated that useful accomplishment with the more inconvenient one of sniping. Anyhow, one could hear the five shots of a Mannlicher at regular intervals, certainly not outside the Settlement. I never heard definitely that any were caught, for they seemed to be mostly in the French Concession, where none of us could seek them; but there was a story of two "middies" catching two lying on a house-top, with rifles and ammunition beside them, but I never heard the story verified.

On the 8th July the situation had become rather serious, for, as we have seen, the enemy had got almost behind our guns on the Mud Wall, making their position almost untenable. The Chinese position at this time stretched, in a rough semicircle, from where the Lutai Canal passes through the Mud Wall on the north-east to the ruins of Mr J. Dickinson's and Mr Detring's houses near the racecourse, about 2000 yards south-south-west of the naval guns on the Mud Wall, the said semicircle having the Settlement for its centre. Making the most of their advantages, at daylight they opened fire from all points, and the duel lasted till noon. At 2 P.M., the Japanese guns having reinforced ours, the shelling began again, the Chinese often lying low when our fire was hottest only to start again with renewed vigour as soon as there was a lull on our side. This was one of the warmest days we had had, and I counted, in the afternoon, no less

than thirty-nine shells from the " Empress Dowager "
pass or burst over our house in half-an-hour, when
I happened to have the time and inclination to
count.   How many passed in the aggregate, who
shall say ?

CHAPTER X

ALL this made it apparent that something had got to be done to check the undue forwardness of the Chinese, so at 3 A.M. on the 9th, a force of 1000 Japanese, 950 British, 400 Russians, and 200 American Marines, set out down the Taku road so as to get well to the south-west of the enemy's right, and thus roll them up. I have no intention of describing this battle, except so far as it concerned us, especially as the official account will be found further along.

We found two companies: Nos. 2 and 3, under Captain Barnes, with Captain Dent, Lieutenants Layard and Johnson, and Colour-Sergeants Young and Dunn. The rendezvous was the Taku road, just inside the gate, and while we were waiting there, the Chinese, who doubtless knew all about our movements as soon as we did, opened on us with shell, without much effect, so far as one could see. In a short time we were under way, and as we passed the General, he said: "You go as escort to the Hong-Kong Artillery and lend them a hand when necessary." We therefore joined ourselves to

61

them, and in a short time they came into action to cover the advance of the infantry. I have said before that you are least safe at the longer ranges in China, and we found it so this day, for bullets came pretty thick round us, which were palpably aimed at the attacking line of infantry, one grazing the top of my helmet, while a man away behind us, with the water carts, etc., was killed. After a while we went on, and as the few gunners allotted to each gun were getting rather done up, and as the ground was very heavy owing to the recent rains, we had to put some men on each gun to help. In this way we passed through the ruins of the two houses above mentioned, the whole ground giving evidence of a hasty flight on the part of the Chinese. Here we saw the four guns that all the trouble was about, in the hands of the Japanese, and being turned on their former owners. Away to the left the same little men were having a lively battle of their own, some of the spare bullets coming our way. A civilian was walking with me leading a pony, when it was hit in the neck, from this lesser battle, which seemed at least two miles off. About now the Japanese gave us a fine show in the form of a cavalry charge among the fleeing enemy, in which they claimed to have killed a hundred or so. They made two other charges, one quite at the end of the battle, when they caught some 500 of the enemy in a village almost due west of the Hai-kwan-ssu, and killed nearly the whole lot.

Meantime we were delayed in our advance while the Japanese Engineers made a bridge for us to cross a stream.   Our guns were, nevertheless, in action now against the Arsenal, and, for all their smokiness and general unwieldiness, they were the only ones that were able to reach it.   Those of the Japanese, which were as handy and as quick coming into action as could be, were unable to reach as far. At this time two or three little smoky guns of the Chinese took a turn at us, from a range of some 3000 yards.   They had the range very well, which, after all, is not surprising considering the smoke we made, and burst shells all around us. It was a curious experience.   We could see the flash, and the cloud of smoke ; a few seconds later the report would reach us, and later on still we would hear the missile come " buzz, buzz, buzz " towards us, so slowly that we could almost see it, for we must have been almost at the extreme limit of those little pop-guns.   We saw one burst quite close to a Japanese soldier, who was holding one of their ammunition ponies, passing apparently under the pony's head.   As far as we could see neither was hurt at all, and the plucky little man simply brushed the dust off his coat in the coolest way possible.

The necessary bridge having been made we went on a little, and came into action once more a bit nearer the Arsenal, the same little guns seeking us out again, though without any damage being done. The Japanese cavalry had in the meantime got round where our small friends were, which gave them something else to think about; but whether they were captured, or got away, we never knew.

We had been having some stout pulling up to this point, but we had a stiff job from here to the Arsenal. I ought to mention that by this time the enemy had had enough of it, and had cleared out of the Arsenal, which had been occupied at once by a party of American and Japanese Marines, who had gone along the Mud Wall while we were shelling the place from the south. The course being therefore clear, a general advance was made. The ground it was our luck to strike, was a regular quagmire, being ploughed fields saturated with rain, and, in some places, under water. However, the guns had got to go the same as anyone else, so we set about it. Anyone who has ever seen one of these 2.5-inch M.-L. guns on its three-foot-nothing wheels will readily realise how soon it gets clogged up with dirt, especially when it sinks a foot or more into it. For half-a-mile or so we struggled along

through this Slough of Despond, things becoming
worse every minute, till at last every available
man had to be put on to each gun in turn. We
finally got on to the road leading north through
the Arsenal to the south gate of the city, when
things were better, although the mass of mud on
the gun-wheels made our progress very slow and
hard. All the same, we got to the Arsenal in
time to get two of our four charges in position to
shell the city, which was not slow to respond. In
fact, we again very soon heard the well-known
scream of the shells of our old friend the "Empress
Dowager," which naturally had the range to a
yard. We had at one time considered whether we
should hold this position in the Arsenal; in fact,
Colonel Bower, who had come into the place with
the Americans, went back to send out two more
of our companies to relieve us; but it was not
thought worth while, owing to the dilapidated
state of the buildings, so the order came for
us all to go back to the Settlement, after we
had fired all the still tenable buildings.

It must be understood that on the far side of the
Mud Wall there is a sort of moat or canal, and
between the two a path, mostly on a slope of about
forty-five degrees, about 3 feet wide in its widest
parts. Along this fine coach road imagine
some 2500 men, of various nationalities and arms,

E

struggling home to their mid-day meal, and in their midst certain Celestials and Orientals, urged on by certain white men, striving to get along four stubborn little guns and their limbers. The Russians plodded along with indifference, the Japanese hurried by with a laugh and a joke, while a somewhat unmannerly shout of, "Make way for the wounded there, can't you?" betokened the arrival of our own countrymen. After proceeding for about a quarter of a mile, we came to a bend in the Mud Wall where it turned off north, and ended at a moat, across which a narrow bridge* connected it with its own continuation going east once more. Here, naturally, there was a great block, for the bridge, being under fire, could not be crossed even in file, but men had to crouch and run as best they could. In due time it came our turn to get over; but there was no "crouch and run" for us, for those guns and limbers had got to be hauled slowly up on to the Mud Wall from cover, over the bridge, and then lowered carefully down, under cover once more, on the far side. I say "carefully" advisedly, for any slip would have landed gun and all into the water. All this time the enemy had seen the strings of men crossing the bridge, and had now,

---

* A reference to this bridge, and its effect on the French, will be found in paragraph 9 of General Dorward's Despatch of 19th July 1900.

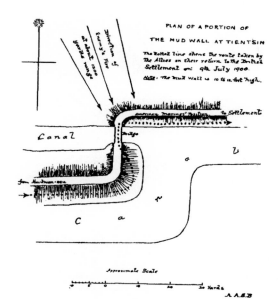

PLAN OF A PORTION OF

THE MUD WALL AT TIENTSIN

The dotted line shows the route taken by
the Allies on their return to the British
Settlement on 9th July 1900.

Note: The Mud Wall is 10 to 12 feet high.

Direction of Enemy's Fire

Direction of Enemy's Fire

Fire from Peiyang over Troops

Canal

Bridge

American Marines' Billets

to Settlement

o

v

from Hai-Kwan-Bell

r

C

a

Approximate Scale

10 5 0 10 20 30 Yards

A.A.E.B.

in addition to rifle fire, brought guns to bear on it
to such an extent that it was dangerous in the
extreme to even rush over it, much more to stand
about on it and pull, as our men and the gunners
had to do.   The men could hear the firing and
see the bullets fall into the water the same as
we could ; but there was never a waver nor a
moment of hesitation as each lot went up and
over.   If, after seeing this, anyone says the Chinese
are not as brave as the next men, he is referred to
the officers of the Hong-Kong artillery, who were
present.   Of their own Sikhs it is needless to speak,
for no one ever questions their bravery ; but our
men did the same, and did it as well as they did,
to their honour be it recorded.

Among all the Sadducees, and such like, that
passed us by on the other side, we had, however,
one friend, and that was Major Waller and his
stout American Marines.   He saw the difficulty,
and lining his men up along the wall beyond the
bridge, he opened such a heavy fire on the enemy,
who were on the city wall, and south of it, whenever
he saw a gun or limber about to make the crossing,
that the fire, at those anxious moments, was materially kept down.   His practical action, no doubt,
saved some lives on our side, and was, therefore,
brought to the notice of Colonel Bower, who wrote
to thank him.   Major Waller's reply was as nice

and as practical as his action had been. He said
that he and all his Marines desired to regard the
Queen's subjects, of all colours, as comrades, a
feeling, one may be sure, we all most heartily
reciprocated.

This formidable obstacle having been got over,
the men were lined up on the Mud Wall among
the Americans, from which position they had a
chance to get some of their own back. Whether
they hit anyone is open to conjecture, but at any
rate they thought they did, and after the pound-
ing they had had lately, it was as well to let them
believe so.

Our troubles were by no means ended yet, for
we had still a mile or more of this sloping path
to get over, to say nothing of the pull through
the Settlement to the artillery barracks,—another
mile at least. It is not too much to say that
the heat and labour of the day had by this time
quite knocked out the ridiculously small gun-
teams of Indian soldiers, so that our men had to
bring the guns in themselves, more or less
unaided. Luckily, as we saw at our first
arrival at Tientsin, the Celestial is a stout fellow,
and so was able to compete at a task that few
others could have taken on in that trying heat,
landing the guns, to the eternal gratitude of the
officers, at the Royal Artillery barracks. Major St

John, the Commander, Royal Artillery, took the opportunity of writing a very nice letter to Colonel Bower on the subject, wherein he said many nice things, which, after all, he need not have done, as we merely obeyed orders, unless he had been convinced that our men's work fully deserved it.

The illustrated papers at home, or rather, the *Graphic* and *Daily Graphic*, gave vivid illustrations of the scene crossing that bridge with the guns, which were wonderfully accurate as regards local colour and surroundings; but, unluckily, put all the soldiers in as Indians, whereas, as has been said here, and as they themselves had it in their letterpress, our men more than lent a hand. No doubt it was thought that an Indian soldier, a more or less familiar feature in modern illustrated journalism, would look far more true to nature, and would be far more taking to the public eye than an unknown quantity like a man of the Chinese regiment.

It was curious that in all that hot fire on the bridge they only managed to hit two men of our party, and they were two Chinese who were carrying a stretcher, one of whom was killed and the other very badly wounded. Besides these, one man of No. 2 was hit in the stomach by either a shell or a fragment of stone, while we were in the Arsenal. He was really saved from a more severe wound by a dollar piece which he had in his pocket, and which was bent entirely out of shape.

This battle, important as it was in its results to us, was more of a spectacle than a hard fight. In fact, it was just like a very stiff field-day, with bullets and shell thrown in. There was the regular good old artillery duel, the main infantry advance, the flank attack, the cavalry charge, all, of course, on a large scale, and repeated more than once, and, finally, the race home to dinner, in which, as I have tried to hint, we were a very easy last.

General Dorward wrote : " 13. The most arduous work of the day was done by the Chinese regiment, who, as escort to the guns, worked indefatigably in getting them over broken and swampy country."

It was a great day for us, showing as it did, how our men combine solid pluck with solid endurance under most trying circumstances.

CHAPTER XI

THE treatment they had received had the effect of keeping our friends the enemy very quiet the next day, for they left us in peace, though some stir was seen about the Hai-kwan-ssu, as if they had some new card up their sleeve.

There was an order for an attack on the city from the Russian side on the 11th, and about 1 A.M. the troops, including two of our companies, began to get under way. They only got as far as the Russian camp, however, when the Russians, having kept them waiting ever so long, said that as they could not get their pontoons, which were to carry the Allies over the Lutai Canal, or the carts intended for the job, the expedition must be off. We so often hear how foolish we are at the game of war, but I am very sure no British officer would ever make such an error as this. However, there was no help for it, and everyone came sadly back. The Chinese, as usual, had full information of this move, but not of its postponement, so at 3 A.M. on the 12th, they made their most determined attack on the station, as well as on the western defences.

At this time there was an order that the garrison

71

orderly officer was to sleep in the Temperance Hall (condemned as a health resort, as has been said), with orders to use his discretion as to having the barricades reinforced, should a more than usually vigorous attack be made. It happened that on this night the duty fell to my lot, and when I arrived there about 10 P.M. one of the two sailors, who manned the 9-pounder gun there, came to me in some anxiety and said that the usual piquet had been withdrawn, and that only he and his mate were there to guard this point. To save trouble, I went and got out a corporal and six men of my company, to find a sentry on each barricade.

About 3 A.M. I was awakened by the most diabolical noise of the firing of every imaginable sort of firearm, fire-cracker, and cannon, and so got out into the street as soon as I could. It was lucky I did, for I had hardly done so, when a shell came in and burst not two yards from the sofa I had been lying on. I found the two sailors and my own men already in position behind the outer barricade, and so, having sent two men to watch the Taku road one, I waited developments. Nor had I long to tarry. In a few minutes the shells began to hum about us, crashing into the Temperance Hall and the high houses south of it with a frequency that was disconcerting. Very soon, too, from the west and west-south-west came a hail of bullets, and we could see the flashes of the rifles among the ruins out that way, coming nearer and nearer in a way that betokened a more than ordinary attack or demonstration. On they came closer and closer, while the bullets whistled and the shells shrieked and hummed overhead. There is no more ghastly sound than a shell, which has lost its fuse, makes as it goes singing and whirling through the air above you, and quite a number seemed to suffer that way this night. Things were getting to look serious ; in fact, the head sailor had just said : " They seem to be getting a bit too close," when round the corner to our left rear, or south-east of us, we heard the welcome rattle of the maxim ; while a few minutes later another arrived, under Lieutenant Lewis, at our very barricade. A little of this soon persuaded the Chinese to go away, and they drifted off towards the French lines on the Taku road, where they seemed to get another warm reception. It will be readily seen that we were glad to see and hear our old friends the maxims, which we had no idea were anywhere near us, as they had gone off in the night across the river to the Russian camp, only to return, with the remainder of the force, as has been related, the expedition being off. They came at just the right time, for, although reinforcements in the shape of some fifty men of the Royal Engineers and our own men, were either close at hand or on the way, the barricade was so short that only fifteen or twenty rifles could be used at once, and a maxim was just the thing.

That corporal and those six men behaved with the greatest coolness and courage, never showing the least sign of flinching, but fired away at the flashes as calmly as the two blue-jackets with them; and the place was not far removed from being a "tight" one.

This was a great day all over our defences, for it is plain that the enemy, counting on most of the force being out of the Settlement, had determined on a finishing stroke.   At the station many of them actually got into the trucks in rear of the main defence line and were only ejected at the point of the bayonet by the men of the Hong-Kong regiment, who behaved with a courage that elicited great praise from the foreign officers there.

To make matters a little more even the city was very heavily shelled at 1 P.M., a new element being introduced on our side by a 4-inch gun from H.M.S. *Algerine,* which, posted at the south end of Meadows Road, about 500 or 600 yards behind the other guns, fired Lyddite shells for the first time, with considerable effect, if the dust and smoke that resulted, went for anything. The Chinese reply was rather feeble.

CHAPTER XII

BESIDES the guns on the Mud Wall we had mounted another 4-inch and a 12-pounder behind the raised road leading to the Peiyang or Eastern Arsenal, so that our artillery was more than a match for that of the enemy. It was therefore decided that the time had come for the city to be taken, the first step towards relieving the Europeans besieged in Peking.

Accordingly, at 3 A.M. on the 13th, the force on our side, in conjunction with a Russian force on the north-east, paraded for this grand attack, and, moving over much the same ground as we had done on the 9th, worked round near to the Western Arsenal, with, however, hardly any opposition at all except on the extreme left. We were on this occasion represented by Nos. 4 and 5 Companies, under Captain Watson, with Captains Hill and Fairfax, Lieutenant Bray, and Colour-Sergeant Purdon.

In crossing the plain from the south towards the Arsenal and Mud Wall the force came under a fairly heavy fire, both shell and rifle, from the city walls. The force halted for about one hour

75

on the plain south of the Hai-kwan-ssu, and it was here, and during the subsequent advance, that the first losses occurred, the Naval Brigade suffering severely. Heavy artillery fire now began on our side, and the detachment closed up to the cover of the Arsenal, where it remained till about noon, when it took part in the general advance on the city, caused by an erroneous report that the Japanese had effected an entrance. That this report was erroneous was soon proved by the heavy fire from the city wall, and a halt was ordered. The party was now divided. Captains Watson and Hill took cover in some houses on the main road midway between the Arsenal and the city, while Lieutenant Bray remained, with half of No. 4, just outside the Arsenal, having been detailed as personal escort to General Dorward.

By this time Major Pereira, with No. 7, had arrived and formed up on the right of Lieutenant Bray, establishing a collecting station for the wounded he had been ordered to bring in, and it was here that he was slightly wounded, two or three of his men being hit about the same time. There was at that time a regular tornado of fire from the Chinese guns on the wall; so much so, that four Japanese guns, which were inside the Arsenal wall, were completely silenced, one being

hit fair in the muzzle.   It will be readily understood that the Japanese, who behaved with the
greatest bravery, lost very heavily at this point,
and, had it not been for the effective use our
party made of their intrenching tools, their losses,
too, would have been far greater.

Darkness having now set in, this party received
orders to return to the Settlement with Japanese
and American wounded, being relieved by No. 1
Company, under Lieutenant Toke.   With them
there also returned a small party of No. 5, under
Captain Fairfax.

Now we must return to the main body of our
party, which, as we have seen, had taken cover
from the murderous fire in some houses along the
main road leading towards the south gate.   These
houses proved a great attraction to many of the
Allies, sailors, Japanese, French, and a few
Austrians, who made it so congested that Captain
Watson moved away to his right, and there, in
his turn making use of his intrenching tools, threw
up cover for his party.   There they remained
till dark.   The wounded were then sent back to
the Arsenal.   Under cover of the darkness the
Austrians, most of the French, and the Japanese
retired, the latter being replaced by a fresh
detachment.

The Naval Brigade, under Captain Beatty, R.N.,

and our party, now received orders to hold their ground, and to place themselves under the direct orders of the Japanese General. About 4 A.M. on the 14th, a message came from that officer to the effect that his men had succeeded in blowing in the south gate, and asking our men to advance to the assault of the city. The Chinese were still keeping up a heavy fire from that portion of the wall east of the gate, which died away during the advance.

The Japanese now spread all over the city, and all resistance was soon practically at an end, the Japanese behaving with the greatest moderation to the inhabitants.

It will be seen from the above that the Chinese regiment had the honour of being the only representatives of the British Army who took part in the final assault and capture of the city of Tientsin.

Our party, with the Naval Brigade, now proceeded to the west gate, and, after being there for a short time, received orders to go to the north gate, that part of the city having been assigned to the British. Shortly after this the Naval Brigade returned to the Settlement, and thus the remnants of our two companies that had started the previous day were left, with two British officers, Captains Watson and Hill, as the sole representatives of

Great Britain in Tientsin city. While here, and before the rest of the regiment arrived, they were exposed to some sniping from some Boxer barracks near by, which are referred to later on.

It was during the advance to the houses where Captain Watson and his party took cover for the greater part of that eventful day that Colour-Sergeant Purdon was shot through the leg. Our total losses were: killed, one officer and three men; wounded, one officer, one British non-commissioned officer, and thirteen men, one of whom died.

We cannot all be in every battle, so it was my fate to be a more or less passive spectator of this one, and it was a sight worth seeing. From the crenelated walls of the city, and from every house and ruin beneath them, came the puffs of blue smoke made by the smoky powder two-man gingals, giving the whole thing the appearance of a battle in the Middle Ages. All this time our guns, which had the range to a nicety, were sweeping great chunks off the top of the city wall, with, no doubt, a due portion of its defenders, but the fire never seemed to slacken, or give the Allies a chance to get up to the wall. As the evening approached a certain gloom seemed to come over the Settlement, and there were those that pointed to the day and the date as an indication of failure—it was Friday the 13th—though their pessimism was quite at fault.

It was, however, a dismal day, for all the time there came in a mournful procession of wounded, British, American, and Japanese, in stretchers, in carts, in rickshas, and hobbling painfully along, which told its own tale of the desperate fighting among those ruins.

In the afternoon General Dorward sent in for two or more of our companies, with all the available stretchers, and Nos. 1 and 7, under Major Pereira, with Captain Toke and Lieutenant Brooke, and, after a while, No. 6, under Captain Ollivant, went out. Theirs was no brilliant feat of arms, where men, carried away by the excitement of our animal nature, do deeds that live in the history of their race, but a series of feats of the truest heroism, the patient and calm collection of their wounded comrades, without a chance to fire a shot in return. No truer valour than this exists. Said *The Times* correspondent: " Whatever the future may show as regards the active fighting qualities of the 1st Chinese Regiment, they certainly possess in a highly-developed degree the quality of passive courage," and he also refers to what they and the naval party did as " splendid work."

It was about this time that one of the bravest acts among many was performed by Captain Ollivant. The 9th United States Infantry was reported to be short of ammunition, and he was sent out with

The engine shed at Tientsin railway station, after the siege. The side in shadow directly faced the enemy's attacks.

a supply, on a mule led by one of our men, for he would take no more. The little party had not gone far when the man was shot dead. Captain Ollivant then took the mule himself, which was also shot almost at once. With no thought of turning back— he had had his orders—he then essayed to carry some of the load himself, for he was a very powerful man. The Fates, however, were against him, and he had only gone a few steps when he was shot through the head. We laid him quietly to rest the next day, in the little cemetery near the Recreation Ground. His loss was very keenly felt by us all, for his genial good heart and his cheery, never-failing sweetness of disposition had endeared him to us all.

To us—Nos. 2 and 3 Companies—on piquet at the Recreation Ground, it was an anxious time, more especially when night came on, and the odds and ends of wounded and sick who came by, depressed and shaken by their sufferings, assured us that the force was going to be withdrawn at nightfall. We could guess that if this was done the enemy would not be slow to discover the move and to follow up the retiring troops, which, in the dark, would have made it hard to distinguish friend from foe. However, as is well known, that retirement never came off, the troops holding their ground.

During the night the greater part of the Chinese

F

troops seem to have made good their escape, and
the few that put up a last despairing fight next
morning were probably the local men and some of
the more fanatical Boxers.

Shortly after 3 A.M. on the 14th, the Japanese
Engineers, who had been busy at a bridge over
the moat running along near the south wall of the
city, got across and blew in the south gate, and
after an hour or so of street fighting Tientsin city
was ours, and the tide had turned in favour of
the forces of Christendom.   It is none of my intention, nor does it properly come within the four
corners of this dry record of facts as they came
before me, to moralise; but one cannot refrain
from a glance at the results of this great victory,
bought as it was at such a heavy price.   Without
doubt the teeming millions of China were watching, with eager eyes, for the outcome of this
rude arbitrament of war, either to rise in their
strength and expel the "foreign devil" once and
for all, or to lie low, perhaps, for another opportunity.   Nor must we forget the anxiety of Europe,
either merely commercially, or for the safety of
friends, not only in Peking and Tientsin, but all
over China.   The issue was, of a truth, far more
momentous than can be gauged by the blood that
was shed to bring it about.

As a recognition of the services of the regiment

through this stirring time, culminating as it did in our appearance at the final assault and capture of the city, it has been authorised to wear as its badge, a representation of Tientsin city gate, inscribed " Tientsin."

I have before this referred to the danger to those in rear, from fire directed at those nearer the enemy. There was a good instance of this while our party and the rest of the British force was lying down, as stated, on the plain south of the Hai-kwan-ssu, in the earlier part of this action.   The force was absolutely hidden from the city wall, from which it was, at the very least, 1700 yards distant ; but still, as I have said, the Naval Brigade lost heavily, while we had one man killed and one wounded, by fire undoubtedly directed at the Japanese between the city wall and the Mud Wall.

PART III

AFTER TIENTSIN CITY FELL

CHAPTER XIII

BEFORE going on to recount the doings of the regiment after the city was in our hands, it is as well to glance at one or two of the facts that were borne in upon us, and to hear a few of the stories with which we were regaled.

The most salient fact, and one that was most prominently brought to our notice, was, no doubt, the excellence of the Chinese gunners. There were several solutions offered. One was that before hostilities actually broke out, the Chinese forcibly detained eight of their Russian gunnery instructors, and compelled them, at the point of the bayonet, to lay their guns for them. It was even asserted one day that one of these luckless individuals had escaped into the Russian camp, more dead than alive, with the story of his woes; but I never saw him, nor heard the story actually verified. What is more likely is this explanation:

that most of the foreign-trained gunners from the Taku forts made their way, when these fell, to Tientsin, and served the guns there with that accuracy of which we had daily demonstration. That Tientsin Settlement was overrun with spies I have already mentioned, and these men, no doubt, gave their friends in the city early and very accurate information of all our plans, our movements, and the exact position of all our guns, which made it an easy matter for the enemy, with their accurate maps and knowledge of the ground, to make things lively for us.

Another thing, rather of a pantomimic order, was the love of the Chinese for fire-crackers. I have already mentioned the danger of being in reserve in the attacks, owing to the almost chronic oversighting of the enemy's rifles; but there was another advantage in close quarters, and that was that when you got there the Chinese would go away, having lighted a big train of these noisy but harmless weapons of defence, in the hopes of frightening you.

In spite of all this, there were many instances where the Chinese showed themselves full of pluck, and they never failed to follow up a retirement, as long as you preferred to take that passive part, or to stand and be fired at. What they could not stand was you going for them, and the consequent chances of cold steel. They are adepts at taking cover and sticking to it, and from it often proved themselves unpleasantly good shots. No one who has served on the same side as Chinese, as we did, will ever allow it to be said, as it is so often by the ignorant, that they are cowards.

We heard, of course, many rumours in Tientsin, but I only propose to refer to one, and that because the garrison of the Legations at Peking had it about the same time, which makes one wonder how it arose. It was that the Russians from Siberia had got into Peking in great force. As I have said, those in Peking heard that there was a strong force of them at Tungchow long before any foreign troops had even left Tientsin.

Yuan-shi-kai, and no one could have acted more wisely, was also the hero of many yarns, and hardly a day passed but he was on his way to Tientsin, or was, indeed, already there, with his fine troops. Had not Tientsin city fallen when it did, he might have been there. Who can tell ?

Having already followed the fortunes of Nos. 4 and 5 Companies on this eventful 14th of July, let us return now to headquarters. About 2 P.M. the two companies on piquet were relieved by a sergeant and about a dozen men of the Hong-Kong

artillery, that number being now considered sufficient after the victory of that morning, and almost
immediately the whole battalion fell in and marched
to the north gate of the city, having been detailed
to represent Great Britain there.   It had been
arranged by the Allied Generals that each of the
four Powers that had had a hand in the actual
capture of the city should take a quarter under
its jurisdiction, until some more permanent government could be established.   In pursuance of this
arrangement we had the north-west, the Japanese
the north-east, the Americans the south-east, and the
French the south-west quarter, each nation policing
its own part.   I must say that this arrangement
existed only in theory after the first night, as far
as most people were concerned, the only people who
respected each other's portions being ourselves and
the Americans.   Our part was almost immediately
filled with Frenchmen and Japanese, the latter little
people, in fact, establishing guards and posts in
all the more important Yamens and places, into
which they denied admission even to us, who were
supposed to have the place under our protection.
This, however, is one of the very smallest of the
complications bound to arise with a lot of Allies,
not acquainted with one another's languages.

Our march to the north gate was probably the
most unpleasant incident to most of us in the whole

campaign.   Once when we got into the suburbs
and the city proper, which had been exposed to
our fire on the one hand, and the depredations of
the Boxers on the other, we came upon some of
the most appalling sights.   Corpses there were,
naturally, in large numbers, most of them in fairly
advanced states of decomposition, and covered with
flies.   In one place we came upon an entire family,
from all appearances, huddled together and almost
hidden by a perfect canopy of flies.   Most of them,
children of tender years, had received wounds of
a nature such as to put all hopes of recovery out
of the question, even had the victim been a strong
man, and out of which the mother, herself badly
hit, was striving, in vain, to keep the swarms of
noxious flies.   It was a sad and gruesome sight,
but there were worse, the mention even of which
can serve no useful end.

We reached the north gate at last, where we
were right glad to see Nos. 4 and 5 once more.
In the meantime, No. 1 had been sent as escort
to a commissariat train which was bringing us our
food and baggage, and having nothing with us, we
could only sit and wait for them.   By this time
the greater part of the city was in flames, and we
were, in point of fact, actually cut off from all
communication with the outer world on our gate,
except, possibly, along the wall westwards.   As no

carts could come that way under any circumstances, and as our carts were in an exactly opposite direction, themselves surrounded by fires, it will be apparent that we fared but ill that night. Much of our time was spent in trying to compete with the more dangerous of the fires.   At one time we came on the outside of a strong concrete storeroom, under which we all were, and which, with its iron doors all backed with brickwork, and its general appearance of strength and security, had every look of a magazine.   Add to this that a stray European, who had somehow joined himself to us and had adopted our own particular equipment as his own, stoutly averred that he knew that the Chinese had a large magazine somewhere under the north gate, and you may be quite safe in assuming that we hastened to get the place open before the fire, which was rapidly approaching from the east, should settle the matter for us.   We eventually secured an entrance, and found that, instead of munitions of war, it was full of merchandise of various sorts, silks and furs and buttons, and many other articles, all of which we had to clear out to see if there were any explosives as well.   There were none.   There was no doubt that the place was meant for a magazine, and was built as such; but I suppose the officer in charge of it had the usual commercial mind of the Chinese officer, and had either opened a shop on his own, or was storing the goods of his friends there, having, of course, issued the ammunition to the troops.

This danger over, the officers repaired to the upper storey of the pagoda-like top of the gate for the night. Before they did so I doubt if any one had been there for ten years, as the whole floor was covered with a layer of dust at least two or three inches thick. So thick was it in fact, that the next day, when we came to regard it dispassionately, we came to the conclusion that it was better to let it remain than to attempt to have it swept away, although, when the wind got up a day or two later, we regretted our decision. For that night, however, we were glad enough of the dust, as it made the bare boards seem a little softer. At half-past three next morning we were turned out by one of the largest conflagrations from the north, coming so close to our gate as to seriously threaten it, showers of sparks falling all over it. We all turned out to do battle with this new enemy, but, luckily, it died away of its own accord.

Those who have not smelt the combined odour of burning houses, burning corpses in various stages, and other matters peculiar to a Chinese besieged city, can possibly have no conception of the sort of atmosphere we were now condemned to breathe, and those who are lucky enough to have had this advantage will not need to be reminded of what it is like, so that it is unnecessary for me to even attempt to describe it.

CHAPTER XIV

It would now seem to be the time to attempt some vague description of the looting of Tientsin city, of which we have all heard, even if we were not present. That the city was fairly and squarely looted is an absolute fact, although there are not wanting those who say it was not. However, it was looted mainly and most systematically by ex-Chinese soldiers, Boxers, and other ragamuffins, who took advantage of the encouragement held out to the inhabitants to return, to enter the city in disguise as coolies, etc., and regularly clean the place out. Of course, it must not be imagined that the troops looked on passively at this, for this is rather more than flesh and blood can be expected to stand. On the contrary, there was not one, I venture to think, who did not come away with one or two or even more, unconsidered trifles, that were, at the moment, ownerless. It was an understood thing that all Sycee silver and bullion was to go into the Public's pocket, some said to defray the expenses of the war, and others, more sanguine and more confiding, to be divided among the troops who had had all the danger and trouble of the last few weeks. I have even seen it asserted that the money has been so divided; but unless it went into the Peking Prize Fund, which was shared among men who had not yet landed in China, we never saw it. So far as one could judge, everyone was quite satisfied that it should all go into the coffers of our much-taxed Exchequer, if they could not have it themselves that is. I wonder how much the silver that was taken out of Tientsin city amounted to, for there must have been millions of dollars there that one actually saw, and any amount more that others saw.

The houses themselves, too, were a sight one can never forget. In some, the profusion of rich furs, silks, wearing apparel, clocks, watches, musical boxes, looking-glasses, chinaware, cloisonné, and other articles of priceless worth, was something to live for and to see but once. I verily believe that one could have taken a few cart-loads of the above-mentioned away from many houses, and then failed to identify that particular house on one's return, for all the difference in its internal aspect one would have made. We had no carts.

I met a French soldier with a big handful of watches, and he thrust two into my hand. They were cheap silver articles, but I knew less of the possibilities in this line than I soon did, so prized them for the moment. Now no man, unless he be a crank, wants more than one watch at the same time, so I bethought me who most needed one, and offered one to my interpreter. He had one already. I then thought my buglers ought to have one, at least, between them, but they had each two, so I gave it up. It seems that my French friend and others had come across a pawn-shop of sorts near our gate, burnt out more or less, so that anyone wanting a watch could have his pick.

Looting is, of course, a bad man's job at best, but I think, when men have been exposed to all sorts of danger, through no fault of their own, from a city that has, more or less voluntarily, sheltered hordes of the most cruel fanatics the world has ever seen, you must not be too hard on them if their human nature gets a little the upper hand of their finer feelings. Besides, when you realise that these same fanatics are having a hand in the game, and will take everything they see, what wonder if you find yourself falling into the general temptation. The looting of occupied houses is quite another thing; but I do not think there were many cases of this sort, although, mind you, there was never any definite proof that the occupants were not merely temporary, being in reality looters of the worst order, but of the greatest "nerve."

I have met people since who have said: "Well, all I can say is that I never looted a single thing. All that I have got I bought from Cossacks and people." There is one quite obvious reply that will occur to most. At the same time, when people take this high moral standpoint, and assert with rudeness and hauteur that the looter is only a common thief or next door to it, it always makes me remind them of what they seem to have conveniently forgotten, that the law makes little difference between the thief and the "receiver."

Regarded from a military point of view, looting, unrestrained and unfettered, is the worst possible thing that can happen to any body of disciplined men, however good their discipline; for with it the common military virtues find it hard to exist, and the longer it goes on in its unlicensed state the more moribund they must become. I have seen officers, of foreign troops, be it well understood, wrangling with soldiers of their own and of other armies over articles that possibly neither wanted. No doubt foreigners say this sort of thing went on in our force; but I am proud to think that such could never have been the case, for our discipline was, on all points, far away above that of our Allies as a whole.

There was one place near our gate that proved

a never-failing source of interest to us, and that was an old Boxer barracks. We got out of it quite a large number of arms of all sorts, besides a big red flag, which now adorns our officers' mess. The place was full of discarded uniforms, belts, and other equipment, besides an immense amount of all sorts of small-arms ammunition. Very interesting, too, were the many documents in the various rooms. Receipts for money, lists of men, details of casualties, and of valiant deeds done by some of the members of this pleasant fraternity. It was most likely a barracks of Imperial troops in normal times, but the number of red bands and trappings on the spears and other weapons left no room to doubt its latest use. Wandering through its classic precincts was not an unmixed joy, owing to the unavoidable presence there of three or four corpses, which, as time went on, became more noticeable and less attractive. The place caught fire just before we handed our gate over to the French, which was a pity, especially as the wind blew all the smoke and stench into the building on the top of the gate.

I have said that the four nations that took the city shared in its government and other advantages that its possession gave them. This was, naturally, to the exclusion of the Russians and others, who had had but a minor part in the show. Well, one day two Russian soldiers essayed to enter by our gate, and were pulled up by our sentry, in accordance with his orders. With a promptness which was misplaced, if somewhat surprising, in one of his race, one of the "Ruskis" fired at the sentry, but luckily missed him. Nothing daunted, our man shouted for the guard, and at the same time closed with his assailant, taking from him his cap and his rifle. The two then made off. Some hours later they came back, and, with every demonstration of friendship undying, requested that the articles might be restored to them. They were, but in the comparative retirement of the guard-room, whence they only emerged under escort, on their way to justice.

We had orders very early to put a stop to as much looting as we could, and to this end officers' patrols went frequently through our portion of the city. This duty fell mostly to my lot. At the same time there was an officer continually on duty, at the outer gate with the guard, to stop any palpable looters from taking their plunder out. Along came a European with ten rickshas full of stuff, and was pulled up by the sentry. He tried bluster, but as the man could not understand a word he said it did not matter much. The officer now emerged to help, and at him rushed the now furious looter, crying : " Ze sentry vill not let me to pass ! "

G

" No," replied the officer, " he is not likely to, for he has orders not to allow any loot out of this gate."

" Do you know, sir, who I am ?   I am ze Consul of Timbuctoo ! "

" I don't care if you are the King of Timbuctoo ; you don't pass out of this gate with all those rickshas."

And he didn't either.

CHAPTER XV

No. 4 returned to the Settlement on the 16th, No. 5 going out to a fort to the north-west, where a large supply of artillery harness and all sorts of saddlery had been discovered, as well as gun-carriages and other things.

On the 17th No. 1 relieved No. 5 at the fort, that company returning to the Settlement, as did Nos. 6 and 7 from the gate, Nos. 2 and 3 remaining there. I found a good deal of employment in the early part of the day, owing to the large number of merchants, mostly outside the wall, who came or sent to complain of looters. I went out with a party on several occasions, and was the means of inflicting summary punishment on a lot of palpable scoundrels who seemed to be not behaving nicely. All these merchants wanted British protection, and as this seemed to be a free issue, consisting merely of a notice to that effect in English and French, and as the petitioners were, to all appearance, quite peaceful and law-abiding, most of them got their wish. One house I visited belonged to an old Chinese artillery Colonel, Wang-te-sheng by name,

and there we were received in regular Chinese polite
style, and hospitably entertained.

It was curious to notice the profusion of flags that
came out at this time.   The most popular was that
of Japan, being the easiest to make : a bit of white
cloth, or even paper, with a red-ink blob in or near
the middle doing the trick.   The three nations
boasting various combinations of the tri-colour were
also much in request, although, indeed, the Russian
combination was rare.   You hardly ever saw a
Union Jack, and when you did it was the merest
travesty of the real thing ; and as for the " Old
Glory " of our cousins, I never saw a solitary one.
Our two flags are so hard to make that, much as
they would have liked them, the people could not
spare the time to make them.

One saw the oddest notices, too, to indicate the
general desire for peace on earth and goodwill towards men that the local gentry were now beginning
to feel.   Some were comic in the extreme, and some
quite simple.   A favourite one of the latter class was :
" Great Japan."   Whatever their tenor and whatever
their length, one could not but note with pride that,
bar a few in French or Chinese, they were all in our
language, or an imitation thereof.

I have seen other reasons given for the lack of our
flag on the streets, but they are all wide of the mark,
the only one being the difficulty of making even a

WITH THE CHINESE REGIMENT 101

presentable likeness of it in the brief time allowed
by the inhabitants' laudable and natural desire for
safety from promiscuous molestation.

On the afternoon of the 17th I was informed that
as soon as I was able to report the south-west quarter
of the city clear of corpses, I could hand over my
gate to the French, and return to the Settlement
with the two companies. As this was where most of
the fighting had been, I foresaw no sinecure. I
sallied forth with half my company on this most
grisly job, but found it not so bad as I had expected,
for some of it had been done already by someone
else. I had orders to bury them outside the south
wall, but, as the ground was as hard as a road, I
had to burn them, in all, some thirty. Selecting
a fine open yard, we set to work to build a pyre,
while parties of twos and threes went out collecting
and dragging these melancholy remains on matting,
or carrying in the same useful article those whose
condition would not stand rough handling. It was
no inviting or garden-party job, and I propose to
go into no details. Near by, in a small hut, we
found a large store of Mauser ammunition, which
had to be burned too; and, as there was no time
to make a special job of that, we just put it in on
the same fire in small quantities. Most of the
corpses had other cartridges on them, so that at
times there was such a fusilade as to bring the

French and Americans to the wall of the city to
see if a fresh battle had begun. Some enterprising
foreign gentleman came and took a couple of
photographs of this attractive scene, but I have
never come across any result in publication.

That afternoon, having fulfilled the conditions of
our return, we handed our gate over to the French,
and returned to our former place. Never having
been much in the habit of handing gates over to
foreign powers, I was in some trepidation as to my
ability to carry out the correct procedure. However, on approaching my relief on the matter, he
put an end to my fears by announcing his wish for
"*pas de cérémonie,*" so that he and his lot just came
in and we went out, with no fuss, the flags being
changed in the same simple way.

We were a curious procession that came in that
day. I have said that we had been stopping all
looting, and this naturally meant the amassing of
a large amount of loot that had been taken from
its unlawful owners at the gate. This we did not
hand over with the post. Some carts had been
sent out for our kits, and in addition to these, we
commandeered a long string of rickshas — labour
was cheap in those days—and set out. What with
carts, coolies, and rickshas, I think that, without
exaggeration, our column was over a mile long, and
a tedious job it was to get them along. However,

we arrived at last, and very glad we all were to get out of that city, with its smells, its sights, and its vermin.

On the 19th the first of the troops from India arrived, in the form of a party of the 7th Bengal Infantry.

The following day, the war being over for the present, we once more resumed our daily drill-parades, which did not come amiss, for the majority of our men were not far removed from being raw recruits, and there was no reason that their legitimate instruction should not be continued.

CHAPTER XVI

THAT night, about ten o'clock, General Dorward came round and told the Colonel he wanted one company, with three officers, to go down the river next morning, with a small party of the navy, to collect as many junks as possible for the advance on Peking. No. 2 was told off for this duty, Captain Fairfax being attached to make up the required complement of officers.

We left the Bund next morning at 7, the party consisting, in addition to us three, of Lieutenant Borrett, R.N., Mr Smith of the Consulate, and a midshipman, who was in charge of the steamboat, and went down river about ten miles, till we came to an immense park of junks. Here we established our headquarters in a convenient house - boat of sorts that we found there, and began our work.

We had hardly arrived when a sad accident occurred to one of my men, called Sung-te-gung. He was bathing, it seemed, some way from one of the farthest junks, when he was seen to throw up his hands and sink. The current was very strong at the time, so that he must have been carried down at once. It was some time before we heard of the case, and though we then went a long way down the river, we could find no trace of the body.

It was on this occasion that our men proved their immense value to the force, for in the four days we were employed on this duty we sent up close on one hundred junks of large size, with boatmen and all appliances, a feat that no one not speaking the language could have done. Our men, after a little, inspired the villagers and others with great confidence, so much so that large numbers naturally preferred to take service willingly with us and be certain of pay, rations, and good treatment (points on all of which our men were well able to reassure them), to continuing their present riparian existence with no certainty of any of these good things, and the constant risk of visits, the reverse of friendly, from other less well-disposed "foreign devils." Naturally, all our crews were not entirely volunteers, some requiring a little more or less gentle persuasion to get them to join our glad throng, and to remain once they had come, but the majority were quite glad of the chance.

We suffered a good deal of discomfort from the heat and the plague of flies while thus employed, because our work naturally necessitated our being out in the open air all day. We found the decks of the junks no pleasant place to walk on, exposed as they were to that burning sun all day.

Not only did the men prove themselves of much value as persuaders of the people, but many of them were quite able to manage the junks themselves, an ability which was often very useful.

CHAPTER XVII

WE returned to Tientsin on the 24th, and found things much as we had left them, except that a good many reinforcements had been arriving all the time. There was much talk about the coming advance on Peking, but it is not necessary for me to go into the labyrinth of reasons and arguments as to the delays that they say arose. Suffice it to say that the expedition was not yet.

On the 27th July General Sir Alfred Gaselee arrived. A guard of honour of No. 2 Company, with some of No. 4, was detailed to attend at the Bund to receive him; but, owing to a mistake in the announcement of his arrival to the military authorities, he had arrived before we fell in. However, we marched to his temporary quarters, where the usual ceremonies were gone through. He inspected the men, and asked many questions about them, and the regiment in general.

It seems that the coolies and boatmen we had procured, as above recorded, were not sufficient, so on the morning of the 28th two of us were sent, each with ten men, on an expedition into the neighbourhood to collect more. I took the river bank

107

towards Taku, where were a number of villages containing likely men, while Captain Dent went up the river, through the city and suburbs. I roped in eighty-three of sorts, who were mostly junkmen, while Captain Dent got a good many more. Between us we manned the whole flotilla.

It was about this time that we began to feel we were being put into the background, as was, I suppose, only natural, there being now so many other troops on the spot. We had filled a gap, and filled it, as I hope I have proved, not without success, and now that the main body of the China Expeditionary Force had arrived, there was really no very adequate reason why we should not have resumed our legitimate business of regiment-raising. This, however, was not destined to be the case, for, on the 29th, we heard that we were to find a hundred men to accompany the Peking Relief Force, and the following day Nos. 2 and 3 Companies were warned for this, the *finale* of the whole war.

For the next few days we were busy getting ready, all the time "standing by" for the orders for the advance, which did not come. It is for the historian of these days to explain the delays, which we all understood to be due to the unwillingness to advance of some of the foreign generals, the advance being finally made when General

Gaselee, in conjunction with the American and Japanese generals, announced his intention of going, whether the others liked it or not. This may not be the true explanation, but it is the one we heard.

PART IV

THE ADVANCE ON PEKING

CHAPTER XVIII

ABOUT 10 A.M. on the 4th August orders came for our party to be ready to march off at 2 P.M. the same day, so that there was some final hustling to be done to get the junk, that was to carry our kits and our rations for eight days, started off up the river.

At 2 P.M., accordingly, our contribution to this historic march fell in. The party consisted, as has been stated, of Nos. 2 and 3 Companies, under Captain Barnes, with Captain Dent, Lieutenants Bray and Layard, and Colour-Sergeants Young and Dunn. About twenty men of No. 4 were attached to No. 3, to bring the total up to a hundred.

Towards the end of the long column, we set out on our march, out past the Temperance Hall, across the once shot-swept lands between the old Mud Wall and the city, across the city from south to north, over the Grand Canal, and on to Hsiku Arsenal, the scene of Admiral Seymour's victory.

When we got near the bivouac ground, Colonel
O'Sullivan met us and told us we were to be escort
to the Field Artillery, and that we were to join
them. We were on our way when Major St John,
the Commander, Royal Artillery, told us he had had
this changed, and that we were to go as escort to
his heavy guns, which we accordingly did.

A few words on this most extraordinary unit,
our good old "International Battery," as we loved
to call it, will not be out of place at this point.
It consisted of two naval 12-pounder guns, mounted
on Krupp carriages captured in that fort to the
north-west of Tientsin city already referred to.
They were each drawn—or intended to be drawn—
by four Japanese ponies, urged on by Japanese,
redeemed from the coolies from that country im-
ported by General Dorward, in case all other means
of transport failed. The guns were worked by
natives of India, of the Hong-Kong and Singapore
Asiatic Artillery, officered by Englishmen, and the
escort was found—and more often than not the
haulage power—by Chinese, of the 1st Chinese
Regiment, also officered by British officers. Verily
a unique unit, and typical of the resourcefulness
of our race.

It was not a pleasant bivouac that night at Hsiku,
but I suppose this is not a form of entertainment
that recommends itself by reason of the enjoyment

to be derived therefrom. It rained a great part of the night, and what with Japanese infantry and cavalry running about, and mosquitoes, there was little peace or comfort to be had.

We were up the next morning at three, and as soon as it was getting light the advance began. I have no intention of attempting to describe the Battle of Peitsang, my only comment being to wonder how the enemy were ever turned out of their position, for both their flanks were secure, and the attackers had to advance over a plain as flat as a pancake, against what looked an almost impregnable position, most strongly and carefully intrenched, and which the Chinese had been at work on all the time we were waiting in Tientsin. It is true that the "kaoliang" and other crops gave, from their height, a certain cover from view, but the undue agitation of these caused by the troops advancing through them, at once gave the said troops away.

The Japanese bore the brunt of the attack, and their impetuous advance caused them to lose heavily, and as we came along we saw many of them dead and wounded, more, in fact, than we saw of the enemy, who had either got their dead away in bulk, or had not had many. I incline to the latter idea, for their cover was very good, and they did not stay long enough to lose very heavily.

The first we heard of the battle was in the grey of the morning as we were advancing, and away a mile or so to our left front there arose that lively crackle that tells of an action at almost close quarters. The Chinese held a copse in a salient of the river, but on its opposite bank, and the Japanese set about dislodging them, the fight, from opposite sides of the river, lasting for some time, and, as I have said, being very spirited. A few of the bullets they had no use for came singing over our way, but did no harm. All this time we were approaching the main battle, and after a bit came under a spasmodic shell-fire, directed, apparently, at the ammunition column in rear of us. Our guns now came into action, not far from the copse aforesaid and close to the river, the naval 12-pounders being already in action on our right. I was much struck with the method of obtaining a view over this absolute plain, adopted by Major St John. It may be quite common, but it was new to me. Two long bamboo ladders were lashed together at one end, and the lashed ends raised, forming a double stairway to nowhere in particular, which was kept in position by guys, and from the apex of which an extensive view could be obtained. We had discharged one shot, which was still in the air, when an irate staff officer came to say we were firing into the Japanese. He must have

H

meant someone else, for our shot had barely had
time to hit anything when he arrived.   However,
firing was stopped, and thus it was that we took
only 999 rounds of 12-pounder ammunition into
Peking!

There is nothing more to add.   The Chinese
went away, and we went on, through villages
showing too plainly the scourge of war, until at
about noon we reached the bivouac at Peitsang,
and took up our abode close to the river.

In all their well-intrenched position, I noticed
one very curious thing, which seemed to show
the extraordinary "cussedness" of the Celestial
in the midst of his modern military training.   All
along the river bank near Peitsang he had dug
good trenches parallel to its course, as if he had
expected we might come gaily up the river in our
junks, and afford him some fine shooting at close
range.

CHAPTER XIX

THE force moved off next day at 3 A.M., but we did not get away till about 10. It had, apparently, been ruled that our guns were not to be in great demand, so they were taken off their carriages and packed with them on the junks, the limbers continuing to travel by land. It is no easy matter to carry this out and get these heavy guns on board a junk alongside a shallow bank, but the Asiatic Artillery managed it.

No. 3 went with the limbers and ammunition carts, and encountered such difficulties on the sandy tracks that the men had to pull them nearly all the way, and in places they had to be got along one by one. The carts, supplied for this service, came in for more abuse and bad words than all the Boxers in China. Originally built to the design of the Shanghai Municipal Council as conservancy carts to travel on the flat, broad roads of that model Settlement, the rude tracks of Chili soon knocked them endways. The wheels lost their beautiful perpendicular, and ground mournfully against the square sides of the box-like bodies, often to such an extent as to stop the cart's painful progress

115

altogether. The unfortunate animals invited to drag them soon gave out, and our men had again to "lend a hand"—or two. We got rid of them as we went along, the last two being cast, on the 10th, just outside Ho-hsi-wu. Their places were taken either by common, flat, country carts, or by Peking carts, both of which kinds we were lucky to find, as we went along, in the villages near the road. We all hoped that one, at least, would get the Peking medal, but it broke down about a mile and a half short. It belonged, as far as I remember, to the Marines, who made a gallant struggle on its behalf.

We on our junk toiled up the river, the sounds of the distant battle coming to us ever and anon. No one who has never gone up the muddy Peiho has any idea of its monotony, our only excitement being an occasional shot from someone in another reach of the river at some stray dog or escaping junk coolie. We were very lucky over our coolies all the way up, and none ever tried to get away, or even evince any desire to do so. Naturally, our men were somewhat of an attraction to them, and they preferred to serve with men who could speak to them than with those who could not. The British junks, as a rule, were well served, for, of course, the men were treated well and justly; but I think that, somehow, the Japanese were even better served.

This was noticeable throughout the campaign, not only as regards junks, but in most other ways, possibly because the Chinese realised that the Japanese were more or less their own kith and kin.

We were toiling along, about 7.30 P.M., the officers being collected near the stern of the junk, wondering when Yangtsun would be reached, and what would happen there, when, out of the tail of my eye, I saw something roll off the matting roof of the junk forward, and splash into the water. I imagined that one of the pieces of matting, or some part of the junk's gear had gone, when Lieutenant Layard, who was facing me, and had seen what had happened, stripped off his coat and plunged into the murky stream. It was nearly dark at the time; the current of the Peiho up there runs pretty strong, and none of us knew what its bed was like, or what horrid object one might come across, so that it will be at once seen that there was no inducement to take such a dive except that desire, in the heart of every brave man, to save a human life. This was the inducement in this case. Lieutenant Layard had seen a man fall into the water, and, without a moment's hesitation, he plunged in to save him at the risk of his own life. It was a most plucky act, and was, fortunately, crowned with success, both rescuer and rescued getting safe to land. The man was a

Cantonese, named Ah King, the servant of Captain Duff, R.A. A report was sent to regimental head-quarters from Yangtsun the next day, and, in due course, Lieutenant Layard received the Royal Humane Society's Medal, a reward his signal act of devotion most richly deserved.

About 9 P.M. we reached the camp and tied up to the right bank of the river, there not being enough water to allow us to do so near the left one, where the rest of the force was.

The following morning we moved up stream a bit, and, passing under the railway bridge, moored to the left bank.

Owing to the great heat of the last few days, and to the great fatigues which the force had undergone, it was decided to halt at Yangtsun for a day. This gave us a chance to have a look round this historic place. The most salient feature was the railway line, with its rails removed bodily, and either hidden in the fields around, or in the water, the sleepers having, of course, been all burnt. The most extraordinary feature was, how-ever, the remains of Admiral Seymour's trains, which, as everyone will remember, were abandoned at this point, when he decided to return to Tientsin. There was nothing whatever left of them but the car-wheels, just as one sees them come out of the factory or stored in railway yards, and the merest frames of the locomotives. The cars had, as we know, all been burned, but fire alone could not have gutted the engines so completely. Not a nut, not a bolt, not a fire-bar, not a handle was left in its place, nothing, in fact, but the solid framework and the mere shells of the boilers. The Boxers and Imperial troops who had done the work had performed their job with a thoroughness that nothing but the wildest fanaticism could ever have instilled into the Celestial mind. Every bolt and other movable part must have been carefully picked out, for one cannot imagine that that rabble had all the necessary appliances at hand to do their fell work in any other way. There was the track stretching away along the embankment, and there were the car-wheels and the skeletons of the engines, and nothing else. It was a melancholy sight. The great bridge, too, had one span all tilted up out of the straight, which showed that a determined effort had been made to throw it into the river. One of the yarns we had at Tientsin was that this had actually been done, to block our advance by that route.

We had a great struggle to get the carts over the sandy tracks to our bivouac, each requiring all the available men to pull it along. Owing to his great difficulties, Captain Dent had been unable to get them into camp overnight, and had had to stop for the night some three miles out.

At this place some thirty men of No. 5 Company, under Captain Hill, arrived with a long train of wheelbarrows, each pushed and pulled by three or four coolies, containing additional stores for the force. This was one of the most wonderful items in a wonderful campaign. No matter how bad the roads were, or how great the heat, right straight ahead went this column, passing all the other transport, for it never seemed to need a rest. The Chinese coolie is one of the best in the world, and here you saw his value, for this train never failed. This party went on as a separate unit to Peking, and there, their work being done, they joined the rest of us.

The next day was, for us, merely a repetition of its predecessor, except that most of us marched, only a small guard being in each junk. As we arrived at the next halting-place, Tsaitsun, we had another unlucky accident. A man of No. 2, by name Liang liu, a most expert swimmer, was bathing in the dusk and got into difficulties. His cries were not understood by those on shore, who fancied he was merely someone wanting to get across the river. One of the Royal Artillery junks coming up the stream passing near him, an Indian bombardier grasped the situation, and gallantly

HO-HSI-WU.

Note The Temple shewn is where the Chinese
courier was stored.

The Allied Post is described in Part Seven.

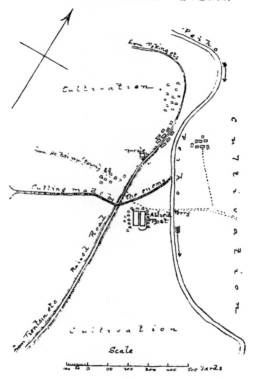

Scale

A.A.S.B.

leapt into the water to his rescue. The poor man,
however, fought so much in his terror, that his
would-be rescuer was compelled to let go to save
his own life, and he went down.

The 9th of August was remarkable chiefly for
its great heat, which knocked out the white
troops a great deal, the Americans seeming to
be the chief sufferers. We reached Ho-hsi-wu
on this date, some of the 1st Bengal Lancers
being lucky enough to come up with a body of
Tartar cavalry, of which they made short work,
killing quite a number, and capturing several
banners.

This Ho-hsi-wu, of which we shall hear more
anon, was, after Yangtsun, the most interesting
place between Tientsin and Tungchow, for it was
here that the Chinese made their most determined
effort to drain the river and flood the country on
the right bank, up which we were now advancing
since crossing at Yangtsun. Had they been able
to do the latter, as they seemed to want, to the
west of the raised road, which at Ho-hsi-wu comes
close to the river bank, they would have forced
the Allies, in their attack on the position there,
to wedge themselves up between the road and
the river in such a way as to entail countless
losses, or to have been content with a distant
bombardment. The place could not have been

rushed from the east, for the river was there, the
west would have been under water, and only the
south remained open, the ground there being in
the form of a triangle, of which the enemy's
position would have formed the apex. A wide
turning movement might have been made to
threaten their line of retreat, a thing they do not
like, but that might have entailed a loss of time,
and it is even possible that the troops were not
sufficient. However, this is all conjecture, for so
rapid had been our advance that the Chinese had
not time to complete their work. We found an
immense ditch, about 1000 yards long, running
west from the right bank of the river, and in it
the implements just as the Chinese had left them
in their hurried flight. At times the river even
ran a few feet into this ditch, and, to the lay eye,
it looked as if another two or three hours' work
would have enabled it to flow there almost in its
entirety. The effect of this on the advance can
be imagined. The river proper would have been
made so shallow as to effectually stop our junks
coming any farther, while, as long as the Chinese
held on to their position, the country to the west
would have gone on being flooded, and the said
position would have had its front protected by a
broad moat. It was a great scheme, but the best
part of it was its frustration.

Except for the cavalry charge already mentioned, none of our troops took any part in the capture of this place, the enemy having been driven away by the Japanese after a brief resistance.

CHAPTER XX

WE now come to the more or less "forced" portion
of the march to Peking. The main body of our
force was ordered to leave Ho-hsi-wu at 3.30 P.M. on
the 10th August, by which hour it was hoped that
the great heat of the day would be over. We,
however, were sent off at 10 A.M., preceded by the
cavalry and the field battery, whom we soon lost in
the dim distance. It had been ordered that, as the
river above this took many large sweeps, which
made its distance from the more direct route to be
followed by the column a matter of some import,
half our party was to go with the junks and guns,
and the other half with the limbers by road. Half
of each company was with each lot, Captain Barnes
and Lieutenant Bray on land, and Captain Dent and
Lieutenant Layard with the boat-column, the colour-
sergeants being also divided, Young going by water,
and Dunn by land.

We spent a good deal of time in the outskirts of
this collection of hamlets roping in all the country
carts we could find, and we soon had the pleasure
of trundling our last two Shanghai models down
each side of the raised road. And it was lucky we

124

did so, for this was a record day as regards heat, dust, heavy going, and distance, and one on which it would have been hopeless to have tried to get those boxes along. The heat was so great that finally we halted from three to five in the afternoon, to cool off.

There was one place so heavy that in getting the field guns over it, the Royal Artillery lost no less than seven horses, and even then, I believe, they were using double teams. We came to the place not long after it had happened, and saw the bodies all within a short distance of one another.

About half-past six that evening we were halted by a tiny village when there was a loud, reverberating report, as we thought, of a gun fired quite near us. For the moment we thought that if we were not under fire, someone at least was firing close to us, till we saw away to the south a dense column of smoke and dust slowly ascending into the air. An immense store of powder had been found in a temple at Ho-hsi-wu—some said it amounted to eighty tons, but one can hardly swallow that—and as it was no use to us, it was ordered to be fired, which was done. It played the very mischief with the trees and houses around, as we shall see when we return there later on.

They had told us it was ten miles at the most to Matou, our next halting-place, but we had somehow

got on a road that took you to one or two other
places first ; for, having marched till 11 P.M. and not
having yet arrived at anywhere in particular, we
decided to halt for the night in the middle of a
" kaoliang " field where the stuff had been all cut
down. Sentries were put out, and everyone made
the best of it. It was funny to see how we became
a regular nucleus for all sorts of odds and ends of
apparently lost sheep to gather round. The first
was a small party of Americans, who asked if they
might share our " kaoliang " with us. Then came a
party of the Naval Brigade, and, at intervals, a few
stray Japanese. Last of all, the Commander, Royal
Engineers, who had been in charge of the explosion,
arrived, with another officer, and shared our very
humble bully beef, and tent.

Nothing of any moment happened that night, but
we heard afterwards that there had been a Chinese
steam-launch and junk full of ammunition on the
river not far from where we were. I hardly credit
the story, as I do not see how they could have been
there, with our forces both above and below them
and still escaped, unless, indeed, they had vanished
into thin air. If it was a true yarn, and we had had
it sooner, we might have had a nice capture.

We got on to Matou the next morning, it being
some four miles from where we had bivouacked.
Here we stayed for the day. We had fully ex-

pected to meet the boat-column here, and renew our slender stock of provisions; but this, alas, was not to be, although we could see our own "house flag" a mile or so down the river as we were falling in to take our place in the column. Had it not been for the kindness of Major St John and his officers, who took compassion on our destitution, and fed us like princes, we should have fared but ill, as we did not see our junk again till the 13th, at Tungchow.

We left Matou at about 7 P.M., and after a weary tramp, with nothing to relieve the monotony, arrived at Chang-chia-wan about 1 A.M. next day, all more or less dead-beat. We dined with the Royal Artillery officers at 2 A.M.!

By 10 A.M. we were all on the road once more, *en route* for Tungchow, only about six miles off. This was an awful march, and told on the troops badly, for they fell out in lumps. There seemed to be only one road, on which everyone had crowded, so that the checks were frequent and long. As the track led through the fields of "kaoliang," which was some ten or twelve feet high, the intense heat was rendered almost insufferable by the want of air caused by these crops, and it is small wonder the troops fell out as they did. At every well by the roadside—and there were luckily plenty—it looked just as if an international post had been established, while any clump of trees, in addition to the well, made the temporary garrison far larger. There you saw collected, in various stages of collapse and exhaustion, men of every nation and of every arm, British infantry, Marines, Sikhs, Americans, Punjabis, Japanese, and Russians. Much has been written about the hardships endured on this march to Peking, but I think this was the worst day, it was so airless, and the troops had done a night-march the night before. Our men bore it all wonderfully, only two falling out, and they only right in Tung-chow itself, where they were speedily retrieved. It was said that as they were in their own country one would naturally expect them to compete on favour-able terms with the other troops; but, after all, the heat was not a patch on that of most parts of India at that time of year, although, of course, no one takes the violent noon-tide exercise we were in-dulging in, during the hot weather in India. The fact remains that our men made a very good show-ing as regards their powers of physical endurance during all these trying marches.

We reached our appointed place close to the river, at about half-past one, and put up in some deserted houses, where we were soon quite com-fortable.

We were gladdened the first thing in the morning of the 13th of August by the appearance of our boat party, which had arrived late the night before. The day was spent in preparations for the final march on Peking, and there was plenty to do. Here we parted with our river transport, so the junks had to be emptied, the men paid off, our kits and rations so distributed as to fit our land transport, all the surplus and not absolutely essential stuff being stored, for the present, in the British Post established there. We also had to find a guard for our own and the Artillery junks, providing them with rations. The heat was intense, which did not make matters any more easy for anyone. We were detailed to find foraging parties to go out into the town, and rope in all the coolies that could be found to assist in the handling and subsequent forwarding of rations and stores in the British Post. These parties, under Lieutenants Bray and Layard, produced a large number of men.

I

CHAPTER XXI

WE now enter upon the last phase of our struggles.
The guns had been remounted on their carriages,
and with them we left Tungchow at about 4 A.M.
on that memorable 14th August. Heavy rains the
previous night had made the unmetalled cart-tracks
mere tracks of mud and water, through which the
miserable rats of ponies tried to drag the guns and
their limbers. It soon became apparent that they
were not able to do so, for the low-lying ground
close to the city wall pulled them up, and No. 2
Company had to fall to, No. 3 being already fully
engaged with the ammunition and other carts in
rear. For some six miles this continued, the track
becoming, if possible, worse as we went on, and
the ponies more exhausted, until the men were
actually dragging them as well as the guns! As
we proceeded the sun began to make itself felt,
and the day to become unpleasantly hot. The
combined influence of those awful roads and the
heat made our progress necessarily very slow, for
the men were nearly exhausted, and it is not too
much to say that few other men, and certainly
no other Orientals, could, even if they had been

willing, have done the work our men did that day. Finally, the foremost gun got stuck up to its axles in some two or three feet of water and mud in a village street, and nothing we could do could get it out. Some time before this, Major St John, realising that the work was beyond both his ponies and our combined men's efforts, had gone on to get two teams of horses from the ammunition column. These very soon arrived, much to our joy, as we fancied their advent meant a quieter time for us. Here we were somewhat in error, for no sooner had they hooked on and got the guns, one by one, out of the mess, than they set off down the road at about five miles an hour, the already over-cooked men following as best they could, for we could hear the battle going on to our right front, and naturally wanted to have a look in. However, it would not do, for the men, having pulled these guns since soon after 4 A.M.— it was now about 1 P.M.—were knocked out by this killing pace, and fell out in numbers; so much so, that by the time we had walked and run about two miles more there was not much escort left, and we had to call a halt by a well. A short rest and a plentiful application of water, externally as well as internally, soon got them together again, and we were able to proceed at a more gentle-manly pace.

I ought to mention that our old friend, Yuan-shi-kai, came to the front once more on this day, for rumour had it that he was going to fall upon the left flank of the Allies while they were heavily engaged in front with the men of Tung-fu-hsiang and the other Peking crowd. As we — the British—were on the extreme left, our position would have been one of some anxiety had this come off.

After a most toilsome march, under a burning sun, we suddenly came round a corner upon an immense arch which seemed to block our further progress. We duly reconnoitred it, and found, somewhat to our surprise, that it was the Sha-huo Gate of the Chinese, or southern city of our goal, Peking. This was at 4 P.M., and by 5 P.M. the detachment, guns, ponies, limbers, carts, mules, and all complete, had arrived,—no mean performance, considering what the men had been through.

Some of us were resting on the inner portion of the wall above the gate, when we were not a little amazed to see approaching us along the top of the wall from the south, a party of Chinese Imperial soldiers, about forty or fifty strong, evidently unaware of our presence. We had only some six or seven men up there, the rest being in the street below eating and resting, so we lay low in order to get the men under arms, and, if possible, bag the whole lot. When, however, those men got some 300 yards from us they halted irresolute, and then turned and ran away. We opened fire at once, and killed two, while others were seen to fall, and then go on again, as if hit. One half of No. 3 now arrived and fired a volley at them, but as they had, by that time, reached the south-east corner of the wall, we could not see if their fire had any effect beyond accelerating the other people's flight. A patrol was sent along the wall, but could find no trace of them, as they had probably got over the wall into the country beyond. Our old friend, Major Waller, of the United States Marine Corps, now arrived with offers of assistance, which, on this occasion, we did not need. We had one muleteer shot dead, through the head.

Portions of the Tartar city wall were still flying Chinese flags, and a vigorous bombardment was proceeding; so our old guns were taken up the street a bit, and added their voices to the tumult, shelling some of the more prominent buildings in the Imperial city, which made us feel we had not laboured altogether in vain.

I cannot close this account of our march to Peking without some reference to the water supply *en route*. We found everywhere wells of the most delicious water, especially at a distance from the river, and although there was, at first, a scare that they might be poisoned, in no case was this done. Whether the enemy had no time or no inclination to inflict this disaster on us, will, I fancy, never be known.

PART V

IN PEKING

CHAPTER XXII

WE received orders to move at 6 A.M. on the 15th
to the Temple of Heaven, where the British headquarters had been temporarily established. Just
before we started, the Naval Brigade, with its guns,
passed through the gate, having had a most trying
time, and being compelled to pass the night out
in the country, the guns having stuck fast in the
mire.

It was no pleasure promenade through the vile
streets ankle deep in liquid mud, but in due course
we arrived in the broad space between the Temple
of Heaven and that of Agriculture, where we got
orders to await the departure of some other troops,
with whom we were to go to the vicinity of the
British Legation. We waited a long time in the
rain, and about 9.30 proceeded to the Chien Men,
or Front Gate, of the Tartar city, at the inner
side of which we halted once more. After a little
we set to work to drag the guns up on to the wall,

to enable them to assist with their fire the American attack on the Imperial city, which was then in active progress. The men of the American battery already there, whose Captain, Reilly, had been killed just a little before, were very glad to see such heavy ordnance coming to assist in their good work.

In the afternoon we moved into the Imperial Carriage Park, on the west side of the Legation Grounds, and took up our quarters in one of the carriage-houses there.

The party, under Captain Hill, which has already been mentioned as joining the force at Yangtsun on the 7th, with a convoy of stores on wheelbarrows, joined the main detachment on this day. This party had done much useful work. The men inspired the barrow coolies with great confidence, and the way the long, unwieldy column was kept together elicited great surprise and much favourable comment.

So much has been written about the condition of the gallant defenders of the Legations, that I feel I can add but little thereto. One thing, however, I should like to mention, and that is the amount of ammunition remaining in the possession of our Marine Guard, who were said to be very short. I cannot now remember the exact figures, but, as far as my memory serves me, they took with

them some 40,000 rounds, of which, on the day of
the Relief, they had expended some 19,000, so that
they, at all events, were not in any great danger
of running out, owing to their foresight in taking
plenty at first, and then husbanding it afterwards.
The food was rather different, for five or six days
more would have seen them on short commons.
Here, again, great foresight had been displayed;
for, during the twenty-four hours the Chinese gave
them to clear out, they had gone out into the
streets near at hand and collected all the rice and
grain they could lay hands on, for which they were
very thankful as time went on—and no relief came.

During the next few days the work of the
detachment consisted mainly of those necessary con-
comitants of military life, whether in peace or war
—fatigues. We made a large opening in the wall
between the Carriage Park and the Board of War,
where the general hospital and the headquarters
of the 1st Brigade were established. We had
another spell of burning corpses near the south-
east corner of the Imperial city, where the enemy
seemed to have lost heavily, not only in men, but
in horses and dogs.   On the 16th Captain Dent,
and on the 19th Lieutenant Bray, took parties to
Tungchow, as escorts for supply columns.

We made some fine roads, connecting General
Sir Norman Stewart's quarters and the 1st Brigade

Office with the outer world, razing a number of houses to the ground in the process.   At this demolition work our men proved themselves very adept. We also collected numerous coolies, to assist the Provost-Marshal in keeping the Carriage Park and its environs clean, and provided a party to go out and collect cart-drivers and other specialists, who were difficult to come at by other means.

We found four or five guards at different points about the British assigned district, the manner in which the men performed their guard duties, their smartness on sentry, and their general behaviour being very favourably noticed and commented on by many officers.

One sergeant and two men were employed as garrison police, and gave every satisfaction to the Provost-Marshal, who expressed his regret at having to part with them when the detachment left Peking.

When things got straightened out a bit, we resumed our daily drills with whatever men were not on other duties, somewhat to the astonishment of some of the force.   Two staff officers, in fact, seeing a squad at bayonet exercise, inquired, one of the other, as to " what they were playing at ? "   They probably forgot, if they ever knew, that we were trying to compete — and not altogether without some small measure of success—with regiments who numbered as many years to their lives as we could count days. An old-established regiment can afford the luxury of no drill during a campaign of short duration, and, in my experience, they do; but with us it was far otherwise; for it must never be forgotten that at this time the regiment had not been in existence for eighteen months, and that many of our men had not six months' service, and some not six weeks.

The unavoidable necessity of looting being recognised, organised parties were, for a time, sent out to collect stuff from unoccupied houses, which was sold at auctions under the supervision of a prize committee, the proceeds being afterwards divided among the troops in shares by rank. As far as one could judge, the loot in Peking was of more value from a curio point of view, but of less value intrinsically, than that in Tientsin. Sycee silver there was, no doubt, as I have heard lots was found, but I fancy this was chiefly by the French, the Russians, and the Japanese. Books, records, pictures, ancestral tablets, and such-like matters of interest to the sinologue and the student there were in plenty; but, as those species were rare, I fancy most of these treasures are still there. There are the usual tales of fortunes made and lost over loot in Peking, but these refer mainly to the more astute, who came up later, and did some good "deals."

On the night of the 25th a serious fire broke out on the south of the quarters occupied by the 26th Baluchis, where some Russians were living. A strong south wind was blowing when the fire was first seen by our troops, and, as it endangered a large part of our lines, orders were given to the Baluchis to put it out even though it were in Russian territory, so to speak, for the Moscovites displayed not the least intention of doing anything, an attitude which caused nasty things to be said about the origin of the fire, in view of the direction of the wind. We were called out to assist and relieve the 26th, and had a certain amount of demolition to do, although the Baluchis had worked like galley-slaves and done almost all that was required, and had really got the fire under before we came at all. After an hour or so we were able to return to our lines.

Many accounts of the Legation defences, the Chinese camps all over Peking, the horrid sights, and the general squalor and desolation that reigned supreme in most parts of the capital of China, have already appeared from the pens of those whose business it is to dilate on such things. At the same time, I do not not think anyone has given full credit to this long-suffering city for its beauty. To those whose recollections of Peking are restricted to the streets, knee-deep in mud or dust and nameless filth, the idea of the place being called beautiful will seem a grim joke. Those, however, who have journeyed to the top of Coal Hill, on the north of the Forbidden City, will bear me out that the view from that elevation, if it can be equalled, can never be surpassed elsewhere. In the foreground the blue-and-yellow tiled roofs of the buildings in the Forbidden City, with their graceful curves and points, form a striking contrast with the duller hues of the other cities beyond, and with the brilliant greens of the many trees scattered with no mean hand throughout the houses; and yet the whole combine somehow into a grand, almost harmonious picture, whose rare beauty can never be forgotten. Till one goes up the Hill of Coal one can never realise how richly Peking is wooded.

CHAPTER XXIII

IT must be understood that all this time, that is, until the 28th of August, the Imperial Palace, or Forbidden City, inside the Imperial city, had been kept inviolate, though why such consideration was shown to the Chinese, when we consider how they had behaved, and more especially how the Celestial mind is apt to misconstrue anything in the way of kindness into fear, is not readily apparent. There were, no doubt, the soundest of political reasons for this abstinence from what, to the ordinary humble military mind, appeared but a just retribution for all the ills and sufferings that had been inflicted on our countrymen and their families. If the usual inhabitants of the Palace were not directly responsible for those same ills, they had at least been fully cognisant of them, and the efforts they had made to stop or end them were not visible to the naked eye. The Americans had, on the 15th, been within an ace of taking the sacred place, but were called off at the last moment, after they had lost heavily; and since then the gates had been as jealously guarded as ever the Chinese themselves could have done.

There were many stories going round the camps about the Palace and its inmates. One day we heard that the Emperor and the Empress-Dowager were still there, surrounded by a devoted band whose last drop of blood would be shed to keep the foreign invaders on the outside of the gates; and another, that the Russians were inside and had ransacked the whole place; both of which yarns were, as events proved, very wide of the mark. There seems no doubt, however, that the inmates held communication with the outer world; for one evening two of us riding along the wall, near the north-east corner, saw a rope dangling from the top to within a few feet of the ground. It may have been there by accident, but ropes do not, as a rule, hang accidentally from the walls of beleaguered cities.

Early on the morning of the 25th a false alarm that the inmates had announced their intention of surrendering sent a party of British troops hurrying out to be present at the function, only to return in a short time as wise as they had gone.

Eventually, however, in some mysterious way, this exclusiveness on the part of the Chinese was overcome, and, to show that we had in very deed conquered China, it was decided to make a formal entry into the Palace, in the shape of a triumphal march, of ten per cent. of all the Allied troops who had taken part in the Relief, from the south gate to the north. It was settled that the nations should be paraded in the order of numbers so employed, which, we all thought, would give the Japanese the precedence—a right they might justly have claimed, apart from mere numbers—considering that they had borne the brunt of all the fighting on the way from Tientsin. However, the Russians seem to have proved their right to first place, although it is interesting to look at General Gaselee's despatch of the 19th August for the truth as regards the numbers that left Tientsin. At one time we heard that the Russians and Japanese would go in side by side ; but in the end the Russians were first, a matter of no little significance in the eyes of the Chinese.

Accordingly, at 7 A.M. on the 28th August, the percentage above mentioned paraded in the open ground south of the Forbidden City.

The troops were all drawn up facing north, and were inspected by General Linievitch, the Russian General, who was the senior General present. This function over, a salute of twenty-one guns was fired by the 12th Field Battery, and the march began, the order of nations being : Russia, Japan, Great Britain, America, France, Germany, Italy, and Austria.

Our force was represented as follows :—

Naval Brigade.

Royal Marines. (Legation Guard in front.)

12th Field Battery, Royal Artillery.

Hong-Kong and Singapore Battalion, Royal Artillery.

Detachment Royal Engineers, and No. 4 Company Bengal Sappers and Miners.

1st Bengal Lancers.

Royal Welsh Fusiliers.

7th Rajputs.

26th Bombay Infantry (Baluchis).

1st Sikhs.

24th Punjab Infantry.

Hong-Kong Regiment.

1st Chinese Regiment.

Medical Services.

Commissariat-Transport Department.

General Sir Alfred Gaselee and staff headed the British portion, and Brigadier-General Sir Norman Stewart and his staff were between the 1st Bengal Lancers and the Royal Welsh Fusiliers.

The regiment was represented by

Captain A. A. S. Barnes.

Colour-Sergeant C. J. Young.

No. 167 Private Liu-chang-chun ⎫
  „ 404   „   Fang-kwan-ling ⎬ No. 2 Company.
  „ 407   „   Wang-te-sheng ⎪
  „ 601   „   Liu-hung-kwei ⎭

K

No. 200	Private	Tung-chang-chu	} No. 3 Company.
„ 239	„	Wang-chen-pao	
„ 504	„	Hsung-ching-chi	No. 4 Company.
„ 438	„	Yang-wei-ching	} No. 5 Company.
„ 451	„	Chang-tze-shen	
„ 453	„	Chio-tien-ying	

I suppose one's ideas of palaces are imbibed chiefly in one's extreme youth, from those glowing accounts of the doings of our childhood's heroes which are considered fitting mental pabulum for our tender years. To my mind a "Palace" has always seemed an immense building, possibly of glass or crystal, with fairies in every room to do the honours, and precious stones galore. I must, therefore, confess to a feeling of great disappointment when I saw the low, one-storied buildings, the dirty, uncared-for courtyards, and the general impression of disuse and neglect that pervaded the residence of the Son of Heaven.

The various throne rooms through which we passed had little of the grandeur that one usually associates with such apartments, and but for the thrones in them, might have been in any well-to-do Celestial's house. The thrones were certainly far in advance of their surroundings, some of the vases and other ornaments on them being especially fine.

The courtyards were really splendid, but their splendour was much marred by the long rank grass with which they were overgrown. Their steps and the low walls round the various halls were all of the finest marble, and were most beautifully carved with figures of horses and various other animals, some more or less mythological. In these yards, too, there were a large number of bronze storks, elephants, turtles, and other animals less easy to recognise, the whole menagerie being chiefly remarkable for the disregard of its owners for the proper relative sizes of its members.

I imagine we saw about one hundred men of sorts during our march, chiefly attendants, no doubt, although towards the end there were some who looked like high grade Mandarins.

Naturally, in a hasty promenade of this sort, one has but little chance to get much of a grasp of the details of what one passes, so that the whole thing is now more or less confused in my mind, though one or two things stand out. One was the appearance of the Chinese we saw there. No doubt at the time I regarded these with some interest, so that their appearance remains with me. Their salient feature was sadness, and a certain smug-faced submissiveness, especially when alone; but when there was any number of them together, as was the case towards the end, as we neared the living-rooms, you could easily detect contempt and worse feelings in their looks. No doubt they felt far worse than they looked, and small wonder, after all.

Martial music naturally heralded our advent and progress. The Russians were the proud possessors of two or three bands; the Japanese used their trumpets, as did the French; while we went along to the bagpipes of the Indian corps. Fine as was the actual procession, it was nothing compared to the *finale*. In the last courtyard the Russians had formed up in close quarter-column on the left of the exit, and the Japanese on the right, facing them, and as the troops went by these two bodies vied with one another in their tumultuous cheers. Before we came to them, the Indian pipers were drawn up to play the troops past, then came the Russian bands, and beyond those cheering masses the Japanese trumpeters, with their slow, dragging time, so that we all had our work cut out to keep step to the various musics so kindly provided. It was a glorious sight, that stirred one to the very soul to such a degree that one wanted to hug someone, or shout, or dance, or do something equally insane. I suppose such a sight can never be seen again, unless, indeed, the Chinese repeat their performances, and so, though the Palace was disappointing in itself, the whole was an experience never to be forgotten.

Once outside we were hustled unceremoniously away back to our lines, while the more lucky, or the more favoured, made a tour of the whole place at their leisure, before it was shut up once more. When that was done, it was a matter of some difficulty to get a pass to even see through it.

TRIUMPHAL MARCH THROUGH FORBIDDEN CITY, PEKING, 28th August 1900

In his account of this unique ceremony, in " China and the Allies," Mr Landor makes the following somewhat odd statement with regard to the feelings of the Allies : " The pipers remained in the courtyard . . . until . . . and at last the Wei-hai-wei regiment, all passed through, all received with thundering cheers, moderated slightly towards the Chinese regiment, for it seemed to go against the grain, even with the Allies, that Chinamen should have been sent to fight against Chinamen. One felt rather sorry at their present position, for as a regiment they are a wonderful body of men."

With regard to these surprisingly lofty feelings, which, if they existed at all, otherwise than in the writer's lively imagination, may be safely ascribed to jealousy, it is needless to say anything, but, so far as any diminution of enthusiasm goes, a word or two may not be amiss. The numberless "checks" and subsequent "rushes" which are inseparable from a long column winding round corners, up and down somewhat slippery stone steps not constructed for the martial tread of armed men, had finally caused a large gap of nearly fifty yards between our party and that of the Hong-Kong regiment immediately in front of us, just as we came to the end. The Russians and Japanese, who were cheering more or less "by order," seeing no one following the party in front of us, as we were still in the previous courtyard, and therefore out of sight, not unnaturally "eased off" a little, rather than cheer at nothing. I know, from my own senses, first of hearing, and then of seeing, that this was an absolute fact, and also that as soon as we appeared in their yard the cheering burst forth with, I fancy, the renewed vigour born of a short breathing space. In all those cheering masses I doubt if there were ten men who knew our men were Chinese; for, dressed as they were, in khaki, with their "queues" rolled up under their straw hats, and nothing whatever Chinese about them, they might have passed for any race, and were, no doubt, supposed to be another Oriental corps. If they were known to be Chinese, which I doubt entirely, we may take the fact of our reception, whether good or bad, as an immense compliment, as proving that we had attracted an amount of notice of which I, for one, had no idea at all. With all their enthusiasm, I do not suppose the ordinary Russian soldier cared a jot for whom he cheered, so long as he cheered someone.

CHAPTER XXIV

ALONG the wall that divides the Chinese city on the south, from the Tartar city on the north, in a westerly direction from the Chien Men, you come to the Shun-chih-men. Here the Chinese had packed a collection of the weirdest ordnance it was ever my lot to see, outside of a museum. One day it was my fortune to accompany two of the officers of the Hong-Kong Artillery to this place to select a piece suitable for that time-honoured institution, the twelve o'clock gun. These experts were somewhat at sea in their endeavours to make their choice among those hoary old fossils; but one was at length picked out, chiefly, as far as I remember, on account of the soundness of its carriage, and was dispatched with humble pride to our lines. We went on to some Chinese field artillery barracks not far off, where we obtained a sufficiency of powder in bags to announce the arrival of noon for months to come.

The day after the Triumphal March was fixed upon as that most suitable for the gun to commence its new career of usefulness. Some time before the estimated hour of noon, a sailor-officer arrived

152

with the necessary instruments to make it noon at the right time, and when he gave the word a match was duly applied to the old gun's vent, but with no other result than a little fizzle there. Nothing daunted, another attempt was made, this time with far more startling results. There was the same fizzle, then a much more pronounced and more prolonged one, ending in an explosion midway between a puff and a bang, and a great spherical ball went cavorting and hurtling through the air, striking the side of the main gate of the Carriage Park with no mean violence. Luckily the rain of the previous night had run down the gun's muzzle, and damped the ardour of the charge therein, which might otherwise have propelled that ball much farther afield.

We had, by this time, received orders to rejoin the regiment at Tientsin, and were expecting to leave any day with the Naval Brigade, our move being postponed for a day at least owing to the heavy rains. On the 29th, however, we received orders which upset our previous ones. There had been left, at various points along the Peiho, parties of Marines, and as these had to be relieved, we were detailed for this duty. One officer and thirty men were told off for Tungchow, one officer and twenty men for Matou, and the rest for Ho-hsi-wu, Captain Barnes being appointed Post Commandant

at the latter post.   Captain Hill was detailed for
Tungchow, and Lieutenant Bray for Matou, Lieu-
tenant Layard going to Ho-hsi-wu, and Captain
Dent being left behind at Peking sick.

We left Peking at 6.30 A.M. on the 31st August,
and reached Tungchow, after a very tiring march
over heavy roads, about 5 P.M.

Before leaving, Major St John told Captain Barnes
that he had had great pleasure in sending in a
report of the excellent way in which the men had
worked, without a grumble, throughout all that
trying march, and made several nice remarks about
them.

It is only fair to add, moreover, before we finally
leave Peking, that throughout our stay there no
complaints were received from any person as to
the behaviour of any of the men.

PART VI

OTHER OPERATIONS

CHAPTER XXV

BEFORE going on to account for the doings of the various parties scattered along the Peiho, let us return for a little to Tientsin and follow the fortunes of the headquarters of the regiment there.

Information having been received by a patrol of Bengal cavalry that some 2000 Boxers and Imperial troops, with two guns, were established in a village about seven miles south-west of Tientsin, a force, under the command of General Dorward, went out against them on the 19th August. It was composed as follows :—200 Japanese Infantry, 300 Native Infantry drawn from the Bombay Sappers, 1st Sikhs, and 1st Madras Pioneers, 50 of the Chinese Regiment, 30 Bengal Cavalry, and 17 Austrians.

Our party consisted of 40 men of No. 1 and 10 of No. 7, under Major Pereira, with Lieutenants Toke and Brooke, and Colour-Sergeants Brook and Bunting.

155

The troops assembled at 4 A.M. outside the Hai-
kwan-ssu Arsenal, and moved off at 5 A.M.   About
7 A.M. a very heavy fire was opened on the right
of the infantry, in the direction taken by the
cavalry.   The infantry at once deployed and advanced in extended order through the "kaoliang,"
of which there were several fields, and which
completely hid them from the enemy.   The cavalry
was all this time heavily engaged and was fighting
a dismounted action, in which it sustained some
few casualties.   Owing to the heavy nature of the
ground the advance of the infantry was painfully
slow, but they eventually came into action on the
left of the cavalry.   Seeing this, the enemy made
as if to stop the further advance of the infantry,
but were met with such a fire as to compel them
to retire themselves.

When our people first emerged from the high
crops they saw the enemy in disordered masses
of cavalry and infantry, doing their best to oppose
the dismounted cavalry.   The advance was continued at a steady double, the Bombay Sappers
on the right, Chinese regiment party and the
Austrians in the centre, the Japanese on the
left, with the remainder in support.   It was at
this stage that the enemy essayed to check the
advance by a counter-attack, in which the Boxers
were given the post of honour in front, the Imperial

troops keeping well in rear. As has been said, a few volleys from our people and the Bombay Sappers drove them off, and they retired on a small village to their right. To prevent them from occupying this village the firing line advanced at the double, and the enemy, after firing a few shots, continued their retirement, with the Allies in full pursuit.

At this point the "cease fire" was sounded and the troops ordered to halt, the Chinese, meanwhile, streaming away over an open plain to a position about a mile and a half away among some trees.

The casualties on our side were, one killed and seven wounded, all among the cavalry; while the Chinese losses were estimated at about 300. After burning five villages, which had clearly been perfect hot-beds of Boxerdom, the force returned to Tientsin, our men having marched and worked under fire to the satisfaction of everyone.

As a battle, this affair was somewhat spoiled by the cavalry, who usurped the functions of the infantry by leading the attack on foot, and leaving the duty of following up the retiring enemy to the infantry, a manifestly unfair division of labour, but caused by some differences in training and ideas on the part of the United States cavalry. Had they, on discovering the enemy's position, returned to the main force with that information, instead of dismounting and getting heavily engaged, the infantry would, in all human probability, have done their own work their own way, leaving the cavalry free to threaten the enemy's flanks and to fall heavily upon them when they fled. This was especially the case, as General Dorward's idea had been for the cavalry to make a wide detour and seize a bridge in rear of the enemy's position, and so cut off their retreat while the infantry attack was pressed home in front.

CHAPTER XXVI

THE defeat above recorded had the effect of keeping the enemy in the vicinity of Tientsin quiet for a time; but, towards the end of August, and in the early part of September, news began to arrive of gatherings farther off than the last. The city of Tsing-hai, on the Yün Ho, or Grand Canal, about thirty miles to the south-west of Tientsin, was reported to be full of Boxers and Imperial troops, and it was decided to proceed against it.

Accordingly, on the 8th September, three columns, under the supreme command of General Dorward, left Tientsin for that purpose. Owing to the large numbers of Chinese said to be in this city, considerable opposition was anticipated, the more especially as it was reported that they had been mounting heavy guns on the walls.

Our party went with that column commanded by General Richardson, and consisted of fifty men of Nos. 1 and 6 Companies, under Lieutenant Toke, with Lieutenants Brooke and Stoddart, Sergeant - Major Cook and Colour - Sergeant Whittaker. General Richardson's column consisted of " B " Battery, Royal Horse Artillery, one squadron 15th Bengal Lancers, one company 1st Sikhs, a party of Bombay Sappers and Miners, 350 Italians, 200 Japanese, and 200 Russians.

This column assembled near the racecourse at 4 P.M., and reached their first bivouac about 6, our men having formed the rearguard. The troops lay down in the " kaoliang " fields, and about half-an-hour after their arrival a terrific thunderstorm burst over them, the rain continuing till four next morning.

The column moved on at 9 A.M., and found the going anything but easy, owing to the heavy rains. After a tedious march, the second halting-place was reached at 3 P.M., the distance covered being twelve miles.   At this stage numerous mounted Chinese were reported to be hovering near, but on the Bengal Lancers moving out, they withdrew.

At 3 A.M. on the 10th the column again moved off, our party heading the advance.   During the night information had been received that the enemy had concentrated at a village called Tu Liu, some miles to the north of Tsing-hai, and orders were received to proceed against that place.   The tracks, doing duty as roads, were in some places under water, and the going throughout was so bad that it was 9 A.M. before Tu Liu came in sight some 2000 yards to the front.   Amid heavy rain the troops extended for the attack, our party being in the firing line. The advance was made for about half-a-mile without a shot being fired, when it was discovered that the central column, under General Dorward himself, was already in possession, the Chinese having quietly gone off the previous night.

All three columns remained in occupation of the place for two days, during which time it was thoroughly gutted and destroyed by fire, as a lesson to its inhabitants that Boxerdom had gone out of fashion in the best circles.

On the 13th the whole returned to Tientsin, our party being put in charge of some junks with the guns and some treasure, which had been found in Tu Liu, on board.

Towards the middle of September it began to be bruited about that an attack was impending on the Peitang Forts, to the north of Taku, in which it was supposed the British were not wanted to participate. This is as it may be; but, at all events, our party for the expedition only had an hour's notice for an affair that had been under discussion for some time.

Fifty men of Nos. 6 and 7, under Major Pereira, with Lieutenants Stoddart and Brooke, and Colour-Sergeants Brook and Whittaker, were warned at 5.30 P.M. to be ready to join the rest of the force at 6.30 P.M., and to start down the river by junk,

L

to assist the Russians and Germans, who were to attack the said Peitsang Forts, on the 19th September.

The other portion of the British force consisted of 300 men of the Australian Naval Contingent, 100 of the 24th Punjab Infantry, and 100 of the 34th Pioneers. The whole party was kept talking and arguing on the river-bank till 11 P.M., owing to the unwillingness of the Russians to open their bridge to allow the junks to pass down. It may be imagined that this extraordinary action on the part of one of our Allies caused no little unfavourable comment and a large amount of bad language. At one time our own little party was told that there was no room for it on the few junks available, and that it could follow by train next day. This plan, however, did not commend itself, and, eventually, the others having started off in a lighter, towed by a tug, our people " commandeered " a junk, and by dint of most determined efforts on the part of everyone on board, and with the help of a gale of wind, caught the rest of our force up about 6 A.M., just as they were disembarking.

Owing to some unfortunate mistake, this disembarkation took place some eight miles from the point arranged as a rendezvous for the whole of the forces, instead of at one only two miles distant therefrom, causing an unnecessarily long march, the rendezvous not being reached till 10.30 A.M. Here General Lorne-Campbell, commanding the British force, met his party, having come on by train. It was found that the Russians and Germans had gone on over-night, instead of waiting for our contingent, but, according to rumour, had been driven back by the mines laid by the Chinese.

The force did not move off till about noon, having to wait for 300 of the 20th Punjab Infantry, who were coming up from Taku, and also for a further contingent from Tientsin. It was a perfect day, and the force marched across a beautiful open plain for some two or three miles until they struck the main Taku road. Continuing along this for another ten miles, they arrived within sight of the Peitsang Forts about 4 P.M., just in time to see the last mine exploding in the far distance. There being no further use for their services, the men were ordered to bivouac where they were for the night.

In this affair, of which the most charitable thing that can be said is that it was wofully mismanaged, the Russians were said to have lost about 100 in killed and wounded, and the Germans about ten, all by the explosion of mines during their advance. The losses on the Chinese side were very trifling, only five bodies being found inside the forts, the enemy, as usual, having evacuated them long before things really got interesting.

It seems pretty certain that the Russians and Germans never had the least intention of awaiting the arrival of the British force, for some deep reason of their own ; but had they done so, what turned out to be a miserable fiasco, might have been an affair of some practical utility, as our force could have cut off the enemy's retreat, a feat quite beyond the power of the inadequate forces at their disposal. It was a curious affair all through, and throws a strong light on the difficulties in the way of any harmonious action on the part of a number of Allies imbued with different ideas and an unworthy suspicion of one another's motives, to say nothing of jealousy of each other's success, real or fancied.   One bright feature there is in it all, and that is the extreme friendliness to us of the Italians, who declined to move without us, and were, in consequence, shut out of the affair in the same way.

The force returned to Tientsin the next day, in two marches.   In spite of all their hardships, dis-comforts, and final disappointment, the men of the regiment marched throughout with their usual cheer-ful endurance, not one falling out.

PART VII

ON THE LINES OF COMMUNICATION

CHAPTER XXVII

We left the Peking detachment at Tungchow, where they put up, for the night of the 31st August, in a wood-yard on the river, all except Captain Hill and his thirty men, who were at once quartered in the British post.

Next morning, having drawn eight days' rations, the rest of us left at 10.20, *en route* for Matou. On the way we passed a number of Japanese with a large convoy, and also a number of the French 17th Infantry, all on the way to Peking. We reached Matou, some eighteen miles, about five in the evening. Here we dropped Lieutenant Bray and his twenty men of No. 4 Company, leaving about 8.30 A.M. on the 2nd September. On the way we passed a lot more French strung out along the road in a way that seemed to indicate excessive fatigue. It was, at this time, popularly supposed that from Matou to Ho-hsi-wu was about ten miles ; but we, who had marched over that road before, knew better, and so were not disappointed when it ran into eighteen or nineteen. The French, however, had not had our advantages, and when we met their commandant about six or seven miles south of Matou, he was looking for that place, and was most horror-struck when he found how far it still was off.

We reached Ho-hsi-wu at 4.30 P.M., and having got the men fairly settled into the huts where the Marines had been living, they going on board their junks in readiness for an early start next morning, the business of taking over the post commenced. This consisted largely in visiting the officers of the other Allies, and in being entertained by them.

It often causes wonder how such diverse people as Russians, Japanese, and English communicate on these occasions, and if my experiences can throw any light on the matter, here they are. The Japanese was the worst officer to tackle, as he had no language but his own. He had, however, a sergeant who could write English and could read written English, though he could neither speak nor understand a single word. When I called upon the said Captain Nagatani, the sergeant arrived and produced a penny note-book, which he handed to me, and something of this sort went on. I wrote, in my best schoolboy round hand: " I am the new post commandant. I have come to visit you. I am very proud to serve with your brave soldiers, for whom we have the greatest admiration." The sergeant spelt this slowly and laboriously through, and then said a few words to his officer, possibly to the same effect, more or less. The officer then said something, and the faithful sergeant traced out something to this tune, more slowly and more laboriously than he had read my contribution: "I am very please to meet with you. I hope you be very kind for me." And so on for perhaps half-an-hour, after which it will excite no surprise if I mention that we did not often communicate or converse.

One of the Russian officers spoke a little French, and although his name was Yakomovitch, we managed to get along nicely. The German officer spoke a minimum of English, which sufficed, and his doctor —when he got one, at last—spoke French, so that we struggled along somehow.

According to the orders on the subject, the British officer was to command the whole post, including the detachments of the Allied forces; but as my predecessor, Captain Mullins, Royal Marine Light Infantry, H.M.S. *Terrible*, was junior to the Russian captain, this arrangement seemed to have rather come to grief. However, as I was senior to him, this did not affect me. The command of these Allies was, of course, purely nominal, and would only have been exercised in case of an attack or of any combined action, and one never dreamed of even asking how the other parties went along, or of attempting in any way to "boss" them. It had been arranged on the way up that each Power should have the Post Commandant at at least one international post on the lines of communication, and Ho-hsi-wu was ours. So far as I now remember, a Frenchman commanded at Peitsang, a Russian at Yangtsun, a Japanese at Tsaitsun, an Englishman at Ho-hsi-wu, an American at Matou, Tungchow being nominally under a Russian General.

At Ho-hsi-wu the garrison in our time was:—

British — one native officer and 35 sowars, 16th Bengal Lancers (after a time relieved by 3rd Bombay Cavalry), 12 of the Hong-Kong Artillery with a maxim, and some 70 of our men.

American—Company "C" of the 9th United States Infantry.

German — one Company of the 2nd Marine Battalion.

Russian — nominally a Company, but often a great many more.

Japanese—much the same, as they had a very large supply camp on the river bank. Their main post was, however, some 800 yards to the north, in a joss house surrounded by a high wall.

The German officer, Lieutenant von Brinken, took his meals with us, and we found all the officers of that nation who passed through—and they were not a few—always very friendly. As far as I can ascertain, however, there was something in the air of Peking and its environs that made them somewhat arrogant and not very friendly either to us or to the Americans. Perhaps it was that after Count Waldersee came, they imagined that they were the only pebbles on the beach, and acted in accordance with that idea. This seems to have been the case, more especially in the later days, when, possibly, they had learned all they could from us, and thought they could then afford to be rude. There is no doubt that they were one of the worst equipped forces and least suited in every way for their work, and many of them admitted that they had learned many useful lessons from us. As we were on our way between Peking and Tungchow coming down, we met a German mule-battery on its way up. As we had halted at the same time we got into conversation with one of the officers, who spoke perfect English, and in due time asked him if there was any news. His answer was startling: "Yes; the Boers have retaken Pretoria." This struck me as being a somewhat needless falsehood, so I went one better: "Oh, is that all?

We have later news than that. The Chinese have retaken Peking." He then went on.

The Americans were, as was the case all through this queer war, our great friends, and for all that politicians may say and papers write, I am convinced that the campaign has done more than fifty old treaties to bring the two nations together.

Both the Russians and the Japanese were too busy after their own affairs for us to see much of, to say nothing of the linguistic difficulties in the way of close intimacy.

CHAPTER XXVIII

A BRIEF description of our new station and its surroundings may not be out of place at this juncture.

Situated on the right bank of the Peiho, about midway between Tientsin and Peking, it will be seen that its position made it a post of some importance to the Allies, for the storing and forwarding of supplies, and for keeping up communications in each direction. It really consists of a collection of small villages, some six in number, which, scattered over a wide area, render a large garrison necessary for its defence. For this reason the post was confined (except as regards the Japanese) to a small hamlet on a slightly rising ground almost in the apex of the triangle formed by the convergence of the road and the river, and very handy for both. The road embankment was intrenched, forming the line of defence on the north and west, the river protected us from any rush on the east, and on the south the crops were cleared away for half-a-mile or so, and a breastwork built at that part of the post. The Japanese were responsible for the northern defences, the Germans for those on the north-west, the Russians came in between them and the Americans,

whose district was that on the south, while we were
answerable for the river or eastern side, connecting
with the Japanese on the north, and the Americans
on the south.

The main town was across the road, and nearly
a mile inland, so to speak, and the villages beyond
it were chiefly Mahommedan, and had, therefore,
suffered much at the hands of the Boxers, so they
said, as those gentry had misinterpreted the absence
of idols from their mosques, and had thought they
were Roman Catholics.   I was lucky enough to have
in my company, an " Ahun," or Mahommedan priest,
besides several other men of that religion, so that
we very speedily got on the best of terms with the
local people.   There was also in the Indian Field
Post Office a Mahommedan clerk, and he helped
very materially in the good work.   I frequently
visited the chief Mosque, and was always received in
the most friendly way and hospitably entertained.
One never knows how much of this is on the surface ;
but I really think that these people appreciated our
presence near them more than is usually thought.
Not only was this shown by the Mahommedans, but
in the place generally.   When we first got there
everyone carried, or put outside his door, a Japanese
flag, but before we had been there very long this
went out of fashion, and was replaced by our own
White Ensign, which waved over the post.   I tried

The International Post at Ho-hsi-wu, from the south-east, British section, with the crowd at the market.

to induce them to adopt the Union Jack as being more correct, but they were not having any; for they naturally argued that if I had a White Ensign it must be the real British flag, so they all duly made them White Ensigns, which I signed.

I have already referred to the large explosion of some tons of powder after we had left this place on our way to Peking. I can well remember the red temple on a small rise, in which the stuff was stored, and one of my first ideas was to go and see how it had all fared. I sought in vain — there was no sign of that temple, nor even of the rise on which it had stood, but in their place a yawning chasm some thirty or forty yards across, and about half that depth. The ground all round was seared and blighted out of all further usefulness, only a few charred stumps of trees and beams showing that there had ever been any sort of civilisation there.

Our little post itself deserves some further mention. As I have said, it was a small hamlet on a rise, and through it ran a tiny street from north to south. Entering from the north you found, on your right hand, the soldiers of the Fatherland, whose few houses had been added to by matting contrivances. Opposite these were the Japanese, such of them, that is, as had been left there to see to the forwarding of stores, etc. Next to them, on the south, came the British post, its few houses also eked out with matsheds, until, as will be seen, we turned to and built. Opposite us were the Americans, by far the worst off for houses, most of them living under canvas, or in matsheds. The Russians were to the west of the United States men, between them and the road, entirely under canvas and matsheds of their own manufacture, although after a bit we gave them a small shanty in the German post as a hospital.

As has been said, the road formed the line of defence on the west and north. On the river side there was a mud wall, which we continued to the south, and round to the west, so as to embrace the whole of our post.

As the weather began to get colder we found that matsheds were not enough for the men, so we started them on to build brick huts in place of them. There were thousands and thousands of new bricks all over the town, which we brought in in cartloads, for we found among our men quite a good many who were regular bricklayers, and everyone did so well that in a very short time all the men had good sound tiled buildings over their heads. It was quite an eye-opener even to us, who might have been beyond being surprised at anything our men were able to do, and people used to come and look with wonder at our works.

The International Post at Ho-hsi-wu from the west, showing the huts and mat-sheds occupied by the German detachment.

The main one was called " Barnes Buildings," on the other side of the front door being an inscription to the effect that the whole had been put up " by Nos. 2 and 3 Companies, 1st Chinese Regiment, in September 1900." Our own house was so small that we had taken our meals in the open air up to date, but now we had the men add on a dining-room for us, and some sportsman found a huge pane of glass which we put in as a window. Unfortunately we forgot it till rather late, and built the wall gaily up without leaving a space for it. When we remembered it, rather than tear down the wall, we put it in at the height the wall then was, the result being that it was rather near the roof. Still, you cannot have everything on service.

We also started to put up stables for the cavalry detachment, but our relief came before we had got very far.

CHAPTER XXIX

Besides building, we naturally kept our men up in their daily drill, but beyond these two things there was not a great deal for them to do. We had occasionally to send out patrols with the Indian linesman to examine and repair the telegraph line, but this was usually done by the cavalry. Daily patrols of this arm were sent out to the north to connect with Matou on that side, and to see that the line was not tampered with, and that there were no gatherings of Boxers. Our telegraph line being an Anglo - American joint affair, the 6th United States Cavalry furnished the patrols on the south, between us and Yangtsun. Besides these daily patrols, special ones had to be sent out at times with "clear-the-line" messages, for these often came through, and the line was often cut or knocked down by the transport animals of our careless Allies, especially in the earlier days, when the poles were only thin bamboos.

At times, too, we used to get scares of large numbers of Chinese to the north, which had been seen by people in junks passing up and down. These necessitated patrols, but they never came

176

to anything. We were also often disturbed by the sound of heavy artillery firing to the north, of which I have never heard any decent explanation. Some said that it was the Chinese troops engaging the Boxers and banditti who infested the country some way from our line, while others, again, said it was only the same troops letting off bombs, etc., to make us believe they were falling on the Boxers. It is curious to note that the people in Peking, long before any troops had left Tientsin, and when, in fact, we were being besieged ourselves there, heard similar sounds of heavy firing, even on their west side, where no foreign troops could ever have been. It makes one wonder if there were Chinese who really tried to suppress the Boxers.

The French post was some three or four miles to the south of us, and one morning an anxious officer from there arrived to ask if we were still alive, and to offer us the assistance of two battalions if we were hard pressed, though why he had not brought them with him is not so clear. It appeared that he had heard heavy firing nearly all night, and thinking we must be attacked, he came to offer his services. It was a curious incident, for no one in our whole post claimed to have heard any firing that night, whereas he averred that it was in our direction. He was regaled with coffee, and went back with an easier mind.

M

There was a ford some ten miles north of us, and we were constantly getting rumours of troops crossing the river there. One party came by and told us that their junk had grounded near this ford late at night, and could not be got off till daylight. Nearly all night long, they said, a battle had raged about them, with big guns, musketry, and all the latest modern improvements. This is one of the stories we used to get, and with which our spirits were kept up.

On the 30th September two Indian grass-cutters, who had strayed across the river, were attacked in a village on the other side only a few hundred yards higher up, by, as they said, some 200 men, and rather roughly handled, only escaping by swimming over. We at once fell in all our available men, but, unluckily, owing to the patrol duty, there were only twelve of the cavalry to be got. In addition to these we had twelve of the Hong-Kong Artillery, with their maxim, and fifty of our own men. I asked the Americans if they would care to send a party, but as they were just leaving the post, and expected their junks any moment, they did not come. I then asked Lieutenant von Brinken to bring twelve men, which he gladly did. We crossed the river, and scoured the country for some miles round, but without success. The cavalry saw in the distance some eighty men, armed with rifles, etc., but they dispersed into the still-standing crops, and we could find no trace of them. After a little we returned to the village, and piling all the inflammable stuff we could find in the houses, we set it on fire. Just before this, one of the men had disappeared, and we had very strong suspicions that he had been killed. These were confirmed by information I afterwards received, that his body had been seen in that very village, the people, in fact, thinking that that was why we had destroyed the place as we did. There is no doubt that all this time there were many pretty loose fish about the river; for more than one unfortunate Indian was reported missing, having strayed a little way off the towing-path.

Beyond this little *fracas,* our relations with the people, as I have said, were of the very best; but we confined our attentions to our own side of the river, our only visit to the other side being that above mentioned. After we had been in the place about three weeks, a large deputation came from a town called Fu-ching-hsien, some ten or twelve miles away, to express the townsfolks' appreciation of the kindness of England, and to ask to be taken under our protection. This seemed a bit outside our powers, but it showed that the presence of our men was not without its result.

The greatest triumph, however, that we achieved

was our market. As has been said, our part of the
defences was the river-side, and just on the outside of
the mud wall there our quarter-guard was established,
the sentry's beat being along in front of the said
wall, where he could watch the river, the cavalry
horses, and the rest of our front. Between him and
the river was some hundred yards of land. In continuation of his beat, northwards, a line of Chinese
used to daily assemble to sell eggs, fowls, fruit,
vegetables, and such things to all and sundry. On
a fine day there would be two rows, with a pathway
between them, and each three or four deep,
stretching for 150 yards or more, containing, possibly, five hundred people, all with something to
sell, and all relying on the protection afforded them
by the guard of their own race close at hand. The
market was entirely under British auspices, so that
we policed it without assistance from the other
detachments, whose men were, of course, allowed
full use of it. There was seldom any great trouble,
for all these men were wonderfully law-abiding.
The Germans had a playful way of sampling a pear
here, or a few grapes there, as they strolled along ;
but a remonstrance from one of our men, in that
Volapuk which seems to enable the soldiers of all
races to freely converse, while their officers remain
dumb, would at once make him pay for the lot to
which his sample had belonged, with perfect good

A scene in the market at Ho-hsi-wu.

nature, for the market people arranged their wares in little heaps for ten or five cents.

Returning one day from a ride in the village, we saw a rather noisy crowd at the market-place, and the market people all gathering up their wares and scuttling off. As we came nearer, we saw two Japanese fly through an opening in our mud wall like shot rabbits, whereat the babel increased. We rode into the mass, and saw, as its central figure, a very drunk Japanese soldier, who seemed bellicose in his cups. I told one of the men to get me his cap that he might be brought to due justice, and Colour-Sergeant Young then sent him home, and the mob dispersed. I sent a note to Captain Nagatani to say what had occurred, and to tell him that the cap and a shoulder-strap our friend had also shed were in my possession, and would be given up on hearing from him, and asking him to give such orders as would ensure the quiet of the market being respected in future. In a surprisingly short time, considering the distance of their main post, there appeared an English-speaking Japanese, who expressed the sorrow of his officer for the occurrence, etc. I had a shrewd idea that the latter had never seen or heard of my note; but, not wanting to make more ill-feeling, especially as the offender had been handled in no gentle manner by our men, I delivered up the cap, and all was peace once more.

A few days later another incident of the same sort occurred, and one of the men brought me another cap. Close at his heels came the same interpreter man, thinking to recover the property in the same simple way. However, I was not taking any, and told him an officer must come for it this time; and, as he seemed disinclined to take "no" as his answer, he was ejected, as gently as his offence permitted, from our yard. Shortly after an officer duly arrived, immaculately dressed, to apologise. He did so so nicely that I almost felt as if I was the offender, but took the opportunity of telling him that, if this sort of thing went on, and the natives were ill-treated by his men when they were so peaceably employed, I should be compelled to stop his men using the market altogether. It appeared that the offender was a cavalry man, on his way home, and that his spirits—and those of the canteen man—had got the better of him. After that we had no more bother at all.

CHAPTER XXX

During the time the Marine detachment were at Ho-hsi-wu their medical comfort was attended to by Surgeon Hall, R.N., who went away with them, and for some time we were left with the hospital assistant who had come down from Peking with us. This, however, was not considered sufficient, in view of the numbers of sick, and, possibly, wounded, who would pass down; so on the 8th September, Section D of the 39th Native Field Hospital arrived from Tientsin, under Lieutenant G. H. Stewart, Indian Medical Service. Owing to the lack of accommodation they had to be put under canvas; but in a short time our energetic " P.M.O. " got them started likewise at house-building, and they put up some very passable huts under his supervision, called "Stewart Terrace." The kahar's well-known propensity for strong waters caused us some little trouble at one time, and we found that a regular grog-shop had been opened in one of the shops in the town. As I had only allowed these shops to open on the distinct understanding that they sold no liquor to any British troops or followers at all, this was

183

rather annoying; so one day I visited the place, and, though the owner protested that he had no liquor on the premises, we had it searched and found quite a store of Chinese wine there, all of which we destroyed on the spot. The Celestial is really very hard to compete with.

Towards the end of our stay an aged Chinese was one evening brought in to our post, suffering from a bullet wound through the body. He had been shot, for no apparent reason, by one of the Germans who were acting as escort to Mr Poulsen, who was putting up a telegraph line on his own account from Tientsin to Peking. The poor old man received the most unremitting care from Lieutenant Stewart and his assistants; but peritonitis presently set in, and he died on our hands. He was a Mahommedan, so we sent his remains off to our friends in the town, who did the needful.

I have already referred to the crops, which, at this late season, were still standing. My instructions were to try and get the people to cut their crops, so as to avert, as far as possible, the horrors of a famine. To this end I assembled the headmen, and pointed out to them the grave dangers of allowing the "kaoliang" to wither where it stood, and at the same time tried to induce them to get their friends, who were all in hiding in

Our street at Ho-hsi-wu, showing the houses built by the men of the detachment there.

the fields away to our west, to come in and cut the crops. They one and all pleaded the same excuse—to wit, fear of the Russians. I assured them that their fears were groundless, as I had the Russian officer's assurance that his men would not injure them; so they promised to do their best. A day or two later, not seeing much result, I asked one man why this was, and he told me that his own father, in accordance with my advice, had tried to come in, but had been killed by the Russians, a statement quite impossible of either contradiction or verification. All the women of the district, so they said, were at that time in hiding in the uncut fields, and one has only to reflect on this to realise how much misery it must have caused later on. Personally, I think the Russians were much maligned, although, naturally, they had some black sheep; but the people had an idea that they were too awful, and nothing could get it out of their heads.

General Sir Alfred Gaselee, accompanied by Colonel O'Sullivan, came through on the 2nd of October, and inspected the post. He expressed his satisfaction with all he saw, and remarked especially on the smart way in which our men saluted.

In addition to him, anyone who was anyone, looked us up either on the way up or down.

Among them, I may mention General Dorward, Sir Walter Hillier, the Civil Adviser, Mr Reginald Tower, Secretary of Legation, Admiral Alexieff, Generals Chaffee and Wilson, U.S.A., General Richardson and the Indian Cavalry Brigade, who made us feel very proud of ourselves and our country, the Italian Chief of the Staff, and all sorts of special artists and correspondents, besides numerous officers with convoys and detachments, either up or down, so that our days were full up at times with new and interesting faces.

I have already referred to the Indian Field Post Office, which for some time forwarded and received letters by British junks going up and down. This arrangement was plainly not in keeping with the usual excellence of the Indian Field Post Office; so towards the end of September a regular system of mule-dâks was arranged, to run twice a week. Each left either Peking or Tientsin in the early morning, both arriving at Ho-hsi-wu about seven at night, and starting off again the next day early, the mules and escort from the north returning there, and those from the south going with the southward-bound mails. It was a very good arrangement, and insured a regular and rapid service of letters.

Almost at soon as the Legations were relieved the Chinese Imperial Post Office resumed its couriers from Peking. One day I received a visit from my

friend Lieutenant Yakomovitch, to ask if I could lend
him an interpreter, as he had got a strange Chinese
prisoner.   There being no interpreter in at the
moment, I went myself, and there I found, to my
great astonishment, an apparently stray Celestial
with a bag full of registered letters addressed to
every country in the world almost, containing, no
doubt, graphic and glowing accounts of the siege
and relief, and possibly far more important matter.
This man, who had nothing to distinguish him from
an ordinary coolie, was apparently a postal runner,
and had been captured by a Cossack patrol and
brought in for examination as to his antecedents.
He was handed over to me, and as I thought his
method of progression was somewhat slow, and
none too sure, for he had left Peking on the
28th August, and this was the 3rd of September, I
sent him on by the next British south-bound junk,
so that that mail, at all events, got down safely.
The man was also wounded in the hand, by Boxers,
he said.   It will be noted that he left Peking
three days before we did and arrived a day behind us, so that his rate was not excessively fast.

The Germans seemed to send their mails per
officer, for these were continually passing through
on that errand.   No doubt they got them all the
better for this plan; but I can well remember the
alarm and despondency that was caused when

one of their pack-horses returned to us without
its load of mails, and shortly after a heated officer
on its track. I do not think we ever heard if the
load was recovered, but I have an idea it was not.

The French mails were carried by the Russians,
who insisted on giving me those addressed to
" Monsieur le Commandant du Poste," but which
were clearly intended for our friend to the south.

The Japanese had a regular Post Office, their
mails coming and going by their convoys, no doubt
with the regularity and system that obtain in all
the dealings of that people.

There was an immense supply of excellent fire-
wood to be had for the mere taking, so many
houses having been thrown down by the explosion.
Of this we laid in quite a store for the winter.
Also, as the people still seemed averse to cutting
their crops, we collected a lot of the " kaoliang "
round about and put it by for winter forage for the
mules and horses.

I enlisted several recruits, three of whom are still
in the regiment doing very well. One, at least,
fought on the other side at Tientsin, but now thinks
he is on the best side.

CHAPTER XXXI

WE must now turn to the other parties of the regiment at Tungchow and Matou, although very little information is forthcoming as regards the doings at the former place, owing to an unfortunate accident, which robbed the regiment of one of its best officers, and the officers of one of their greatest favourites, and almost wiped the detachment out.

I have, however, the best possible authority for stating that the inhabitants of the neighbouring villages appreciated the presence of our men as much as was the case at the other posts, and that the men did an enormous amount of good in the way of conciliating them. It is only natural that this should be the case, when one thinks what a suspicious race the Chinese are and how impossible it is to get them to place any reliance in what they are told. The ordinary "foreign devil" may assure them of his good-will, and may make them all sorts of promises, at which they will only "wink the other eye"; but show them one of their own race, well fed, well cared for, and generally full of contentment, and they must realise that there is something in the ways of the nation that can

189

produce such a man—or a score of them—for
their inspection and examination, that makes it
different to the rest. In at least one village near
Tungchow the inhabitants asked permission to
have two of our men permanently in their village
as a safeguard against both robbers of their own
race and of the Allies, a request which could
hardly have been granted, though at this remote
date it is impossible to say if it was or not.

On the 14th September a large fatigue party
from the British post was employed destroying gun-
powder which had been found in large quantities
near by. Some of it was sunk in the river, but
far the larger quantity was destroyed by the more
effectual fire, it being spread out on the ground
and then ignited. The whole thing is rather a
mystery; but it would appear that just after some
had been so destroyed, another batch was being
spread out by a large number of men emptying it
out of its cannisters upon the ground. Suddenly, it
would appear, one of the trains fell upon a patch
of ground not yet cold from the last ignition, or
where a fatal spark still lurked, with the result
that the whole batch went up in one almost
simultaneous "puff," setting fire to the clothes
of the unfortunate men at work, before they had
time to escape, many probably never knowing what
had happened. The result was that Captain Hill,

who was directing the operation, and eleven of
our men were most severely burned, so severely,
in fact, that all but two men died within the next
few days, the other two being fit for very little
afterwards.

Besides our men, the Welsh Fusiliers had ten
men injured, the 7th Rajputs, four; the 1st Sikhs,
eleven—in all, one officer, one native officer, and
36 rank and file.

CHAPTER XXXII

MATOU, a long straggling village on the right bank of the Peiho, midway between Ho-hsi-wu and Tung-chow, was an international post on the lines of communication, commanded by an American officer, as has been said already, and there Lieutenant Bray, with twenty men of No. 4 Company, arrived on the 1st September 1900. It was the headquarters of the squadron of the Indian cavalry told off to patrol the line from Tungchow on the north to Ho-hsi-wu on the south. The other British troops there were, ten of the Royal Welsh Fusiliers, thirty men from the native Indian regiments, a few telegraph operators, and Indian sappers, besides our own men. There were also parties of Americans, Russians, Germans, and French.

After his arrival Lieutenant Bray set to work to fortify the British section by means of shelter trenches, loop-holed walls, and other recognised methods, besides clearing away the high crops for some 500 yards to the front.

Owing to the orders we had to cultivate friendly relations with the surrounding people, Lieutenant Bray got the officers of the other Allies to prevent their men going into the villages round about, at the same time informing the head-men that their people would receive full protection if they would come in and establish a regular market for the sale of eggs, vegetables, etc. This they readily did, with the result that there was always an ample supply of such commodities, and the best relations were entered into with the people. It will thus be seen once more that our men were instrumental in doing much good in the way of reassuring these unfortunate people, who, in reality, were probably far more sinned against than sinning.

On the 9th September an American patrol was attacked by Boxers, a little over a mile to the north of Matou. As soon as news of this was received, Captain Browne, commanding the party of the 1st Bengal Lancers, went out with twenty-five of his men, and coming upon the Boxers about four miles out, killed about fifty of them, without losing a man.

About this time the same sounds of furious battles raging near at hand perturbed the Matou garrison, heavy firing having been heard in a south-westerly direction. The prevalent idea seemed to be that on many occasions this firing was either the villagers fighting with the bands of robbers who seemed to infest the country side, or merely firing off their ancient pieces to discourage those same bands and encourage themselves at the same time.

N

On the 22nd a German patrol was fired on at a village some miles to the south, and the following day a composite force went out to see about it. The force consisted of forty British cavalry, twenty-five British infantry, mainly composed of our men, seventy-five Americans, twenty-five Germans, and forty Japanese. The defaulting village was found to be deserted, and to all appearances looted. Though cleared of most other things, it contained, curiously enough, a considerable quantity of weapons, including Mauser rifles, which were all removed. Lieutenant Hunter, of the 3rd Bombay Cavalry, which had by this time relieved the 1st Bengal Lancers, came upon some 2000 Boxers, with carts laden with loot; but, owing to some mistake, this good news never reached the main body until it was too late to go after them.

CHAPTER XXXIII

ALL things are bound to have an end, and so it was as regards our sojourn on the Peiho. I shall not attempt to disguise the fact that I liked being there, in spite of the few disadvantages, due to an absence of proper accommodation as the weather got colder, and to the fact that we had but slender raiment. The advantages far outweighed all this. As regards that portion of our anatomy on which an army is said to march, I doubt if anyone in China, on service or in peace time, was better off. The food of ourselves, our colour-sergeants, and our men, was first-rate in quality and quantity, and we wanted nothing except a regular supply of bread, which we did not always get, being just about midway between two bakeries. The place was, moreover, exceedingly interesting owing to the constant stream of traffic of troops, stores, and people of importance, by road and river. It was a very liberal education—as indeed was the whole campaign—on the ways of various nationalities who may not always be on our side, but any reference to these ways does not naturally enter into these pages.

On the 6th October a party of the 1st Madras

Pioneers, under Captain Batten, arrived to relieve us, and we left the next morning. The local people were, naturally, sorry to see the last of us, and so were the remainder of the British garrison. In some mysterious way peculiar to soldiers, our men had become great friends with the Indian soldiers, and there were many somewhat amusing partings to be witnessed between them, although neither knew a word of the other's tongue. It was curious also to see how friendly one or two of the German soldiers were with our men. I daresay they came from Kiao-chau, where they had picked up a few words of Chinese, and were improving the occasion by a little practice.

On the 7th we marched right through to Yangtsun, some twenty-one miles, halting at Tsaitsun *en route*. In the forenoon we met Li-hung-chang going north under Russian escort, and I was able to take a snapshot of the astute old man as he went by. He may be made out sitting in the shade of the junk's deckhouse. His junk, with its immense dark blue sail and Chinese flag, was a very conspicuous object for miles in that flat country.

It rained all that night at Yangtsun, and all next day, for that matter; but as the men had no proper shelter, we started once more at noon, having waited in vain for it to fair up. We passed over the former battlefield, and halted, in heavy rain, for about an

Li Hung Chang en route to Peking, under Russian escort, 7th October 1900.

hour in the afternoon, making an immense bonfire for the men to dry their clothes. We finally halted for the night in an outlying portion of a village on the river, taking possession of a large house with two courtyards, which held us, mules and all, comfortably. As it was detached from the remainder, and stoutly built with a wall all round, a couple of sentries gave us all the security from any sudden attack that we needed. In the evening we saw thousands and thousands of duck flying over our heads in a southerly direction. I should be sorry to hazard even a guess at their numbers, for no one who has never seen this sight would believe me, but they were countless. The next day, when near Tientsin, we saw the same thing away to the north, and they were like great long clouds.

We went on next morning, and after a short halt at the bridge at Peitsang, and another outside Tientsin city, arrived at our old billet in Collins & Company's godowns shortly after 2 P.M. Tientsin we found much changed. The place was full of soldiers of all sorts, more or less pleasant to meet on a dark night, and everywhere we could see the signs of improvement in the place due to the exertions of the local provisional government, at that time consisting of only three members, Colonel Bower, Colonel Wogack (Russia), and Colonel Aoki (Japan). Bands played in the gardens nearly every evening, causing great and notable gatherings of the *élite*. A Zouave band was specially fine and large, and, from its number of reed instruments, was preferred by most people to an almòst equally fine German band with whom brass predominated.

The regiment was very largely employed on guard duties, and we found no less than nine, besides our own quarter-guard. It was this alone that kept us on at Tientsin, as we could not be spared from that garrison until the arrival of the majority of the Fourth Indian Brigade, who helped our old friends, the Hong-Kong Regiment, in these guard duties after we had left.

We finally left the scene of our early struggles on the 20th of October 1900, being played to the station by the band and drums of the Hong-Kong Regiment, a kindness that was very deeply appreciated by us all. It was an awful day. First the dust was appalling; and, just as we arrived at the station, to hear the glad tidings that our train from the north was some two hours late, it began to rain and snow, with that bitter North China north wind, which has to be met to be fully appreciated. The men were by this time packed in empty open trucks, and amidst these pleasant surroundings we awaited the arrival of our train. We were but little better off then,

Halt of the detachment from Ho-hsi-wu outside Tientsin city 9th October 1900, on the way to rejoin headquarters.

but it was some comfort to be on the move, at all events. In due course, after a journey whose absolute hardships no one will ever forget, we reached the station at Tongku, only to find that the Russian officer in charge of the arrangements ordered our engine away and steadfastly refused, for over an hour, to have us pulled to the British depôt at Sinho, some two or three miles away, on a small branch line. This totally needless " dog in the manger " action caused that officer to be regarded with but small favour by us, wretched and cold as we all were. Much has been said about the action of our trusty allies with regard to the railway, but I am glad to say that this was my only experience of it. In due time we got, however, to Sinho, where we found the s.s. *Shengking* lying alongside the jetty for us. As it was now dark, all we could do was to get the baggage off the train, to be put on board next day, and to get the men settled down for the night, which was soon done.

Next day was as brilliant as its predecessor had been bad, and we got away by noon, down the Peiho, past Tongku and its busy scenes, so different from the deserted aspect of the place when most of us had seen it first four months before, and the Taku forts, still flying the flags of the Allies. We stuck on the Taku bar, as is so often the fate of ships in those waters, and did not get off for twenty-four hours. It is one of the queerest sights in a queer land to see steamers of all sorts and sizes sitting on the Taku mud at low water, with only three or four feet of water under them, and all their lines exposed as if in dry dock. We got off the next afternoon, after a great struggle, and were soon alongside the P. and O. s.s. *Sumatra*, which, after an uneventful voyage, brought us the next evening to Wei-hai-wei. We were disembarked the next forenoon, and in the fulness of time arrived at Matou, where no one had expected us, but where we were, nevertheless, very welcome. One can never hope to penetrate the Chinese mind, but I have no doubt there were many glad hearts that day, for, after all, human nature is the same all the world over.

There remains but little now to tell, for since then our life has been one of peace and daily routine, such as is the same everywhere. Early in May 1901, the note of war was once more sounded over some more or less fancied troubles in Korea, and we were warned to stand by with 600 men, for conveyance to Chemulpo in H.M.S. *Terrible*. We did so for about a week, till the scare died a natural death.

All this time we have not stood still. At the moment, we have 12 companies of over 1200 men, and, should there be another call for our services, we can easily find a party far in excess of the little one of 200 men that first left Wei-hai-wei for the front on the 20th June 1900.

APPENDICES

APPENDIX A

NEWSPAPER CUTTINGS

A FEW newspaper cuttings relative to the 1st Chinese Regiment in action in North China, May to October 1900.

Note.—It must be understood that the following are merely extracts and examples of the telegrams and articles that appeared at home relative to the Chinese regiment. Want of space, and a desire to avoid what might seem unnecessary repetition, have combined to make me omit a good many that might have been reproduced, especially from the Shanghai papers, whose correspondents might be supposed by some to reflect simply regimental views. Though this is far from being the case, I have, nevertheless, thought it best not to draw on them to any extent.

Notices derogatory to the regiment there may have been, but it has not been my fate to see any, except one in a San Francisco paper, which was palpably written by a man who had never seen us, even if he had ever been in China, which was not apparent, for most of his statements about other troops and armies seemed to indicate that his knowledge was derived mostly from the papers, with the result that everything was very mixed.

The dates in brackets are those of publication, where these are not otherwise stated.

REUTER'S TELEGRAM (8th May 1900).—WEI-HAI-WEI, 7th May.—An attack was made on the two camps of the Wei-hai-wei Boundary Commission on the 5th inst. Major C. Penrose and four men of the Chinese regiment were wounded. The attacking party was repulsed, at least thirty of them being killed. The disturbances were due to the Chinese officials, who have been working on the credulity of the natives. The Chinese regiment behaved splendidly.

Dundee Advertiser, 9th May 1900.—In the brief telegrams from Wei-hai-wei, narrating an attack by 3000 Chinese on the British officer engaged on the demarcation of the frontier, there are highly eulogistic references to the conduct of the Chinese composing the Wei-hai-wei regiment. There were only sixty of them in the officer's escort, and they faced up to an attacking mob fifty times their number. In the War Office message their conduct is described as "admirable," and the Reuter message says they "behaved splendidly."

Manchester Courier, 9th May.— . . . The one satisfactory feature of both affairs was the admirable conduct of our new native Chinese regiment. Two companies of the force had to stand the brunt of both attacks, having furnished the escorts, and they emerged with flying colours from this first practical test of their military qualities. They remained "true to their salt" in the face of overwhelming numbers of their fellow-countrymen, and well repaid the pains which have been expended on their training by their British officers.

Yorkshire Herald, 9th May.— . . . The regiment, which was only formed a short time ago, stood firm and beat off the attacking party without the loss of a man, although four of their number were wounded. . . . The confidence reposed by them in their officers served them in good stead, and the cowardly horde were repulsed, twenty of their number being killed. . . . A few months' training has enabled men who, before their connection with the British military system, would have fled from their foes like ghosts before the cock-crow, to face odds of fifty to one and to come off victorious. This episode speaks volumes for the capacity of the capable British officer for bringing to the surface the courage which is part of the equipment of every man worthy of the name.

Globe, 8th May.— . . . Two possible risks might have occurred to the commandant of the Wei-hai-wei regiment, when the camps were assailed by, no doubt, largely superior numbers. His men, scarcely inured to discipline, might either break their formation or give way to disloyalty.   Happily, the battalion proved both trustworthy and courageous ; standing its ground as firmly as seasoned troops could have done, it emerged from its baptism of fire in a highly creditable manner.

Londoner, 12th May.— . . . More significant is the admirable steadiness, under English officers, of the little body of Chinese troops who beat them off.   Once again Englishmen have shown their unique power of manufacturing admirable soldiers out of native material, and their success may prove important in future times of trouble.

The Times correspondent (15th May 1900). — PEKING, 13th May.—Much satisfaction is felt in British circles at the admirable coolness and discipline of the soldiers of the Chinese regiment, which prove the complete success of the experiment of forming a Chinese force under British officers.

(Many more there are to the same effect, but the above should suffice to show that the men's conduct at that trying time elicited much favourable comment in papers of all kinds.)

CENTRAL NEWS TELEGRAM (8th July 1900).—TAKU, 28th June.—The 1st Chinese Regiment at Wei-hai-wei at the commencement of the crisis eagerly begged to be sent to the front to fight under their adopted flag, and as time went on without the arrival of the desired orders dissatisfaction was openly expressed by the men.   Finally it was decided to give the new regiment a chance, and there was wild rejoicing at Wei-hai-wei when the orders came to hand.

Daily Mail correspondent (11th July 1900).—TIENTSIN, 5th July.— . . . There is general satisfaction at the conduct of the 1st Chinese Regiment, which has already been under fire two or three times . . . . The accuracy of the Chinese artillery is simply incredible.   Many of their guns quite outrange those of the Allies, and the shells are dropped among our gunners with marvellous aim.

REUTER'S TELEGRAM (12th July 1900).—TIENTSIN, 5th July.—Yesterday an attack was made on the foreign settlement, from two directions, by large bodies of Chinese troops. . . . The British Chinese Regiment was engaged, and proved very steady under fire.

Daily Mail correspondent (26th July 1900).—SHANGHAI, 24th July.—. . . Major Bruce and two companies of the 1st Chinese Regiment advanced with the intention of rushing a gun. The moment he got clear of the Settlement he was met by a murderous fire from an enemy well-placed under cover, and was forced to retire. Securing the assistance of a company from H.M.S. *Barfleur*, he returned to the attack, and although he gained ground he was again forced to retire with a heavy list of casualties.

Evening News, 1st August 1900.—The following letter has just been received by the family of one of " Her Majesty's Jollies" quartered at Wei-hai-wei. The writer says : ". . . . The 1st Chinese Regiment is a splendid lot of men, and they would knock spots off our Guards at home in drill and marching."

Daily News, 8th August. — How creditably the Chinese regiment behaved in the fighting round Tientsin has been told in the telegrams from the front.

The Daily Graphic, 7th September 1900.—A very pleasant incident of the "blood is thicker than water" description took place at Tientsin during the return to the settlement of Admiral Seymour's allied force from the Hai-Kwan-Su, or Eastern Arsenal. The only available road, or rather path, was behind a large mud wall, originally built for the defence of Tientsin, along which everyone hurried in their zeal to get home to dinner. The four guns of the Hong-Kong Artillery, which are hauled by man draft, were naturally the slowest in the race, although a party of the 1st Chinese Regiment, about 100 strong, under Captain Barnes, which had been told off as escort, were all employed assisting the gunners to keep their guns moving. In fact, the 1st Chinese did yeoman service throughout the whole of a very trying day, and by their aid materially assisted the guns to come readily into action. About a quarter of a mile along the mud wall a canal had to be crossed by a bridge, exposed to a very heavy fire from the Tientsin city wall, and some snipers who were close to it. As each gun had to be hauled slowly by hand diagonally up a steep bank, over the bridge, and down into cover on the other side, it speaks well for the steadiness of our new Chinese troops that, although exposed, necessarily in great clumps, to a heavy fire, they never faltered in their work. It is certain, however, that they would not have accomplished the task with the few losses they sustained had it not been for the action of some fifty of the American Marines, under Major Waller, who, whenever a gun or limber was about to be taken across the bridge, opened a heavy fire upon the enemy, materially keeping down their fire. The incident made a very good impression, for, although there were only some half-dozen British officers with the guns and their Chinese escort, the men being all natives of India or China, it proved that the American Marines, as they themselves said, desired to regard all the Queen's subjects, of whatever colour, as comrades.

The Morning Post correspondent (12th September 1900).— TIENTSIN, 1st August.—. . . Such a cosmopolitan crowd of fighting men was surely never seen before . . . ; straw-hatted, tall, military Chinamen, in loose, black-sashed khaki, from the Wei-hai-wei regiment—examples of how Great Britain makes " men out of mud," as Kipling puts it. . . . The Wei-hai-wei Chinamen, it may be mentioned, won praise from all on the 14th of July. A party of twenty-three hospital men started for the point where the Americans were lying down behind the mud graves and dykes south of the town. The Americans were exposed to a merciless fire, and needed stretcher and hospital men badly ; but the American officer in command (their Colonel having been killed) stood behind a grave mound and frantically waved the stretcher-men back, believing it to be impossible for them to come out across the zone of fire. The

Chinamen, however, paid no attention to him, but trotted on until they reached their goal. Out of twenty-three of these brave fellows eight fell.

The Manchester Guardian correspondent (14th September 1900).—TIENTSIN, 14th July.—. . . The 1st Chinese Regiment, raised in Wei-hai-wei, has behaved admirably under both shell and rifle fire, without much dash, but with a stoical composure which is often of quite as much value. The conclusion come to by those who have watched their conduct here in the field is that they are capable of anything under good leading, but that with them it is very much a case of devotion to and belief in their officers.

The Broad Arrow, 22nd September 1900.—. . . The difference between the English and German soldier is not spiritual, but national. . . . The individuality, capacity for initiative and independence of the Englishman have made him supreme in the world ; the German, who readily submits to authority, and lacks self-reliance, has been forced to play a lesser part. Apparently Colonel Maude has mistaken a national characteristic for duty at its best. If not, how is it that Germans so signally fail to rule foreign peoples? Their Chinese regiment, raised in Shan-tung, went over in a body to their own people at the first opportunity ; the Chinese regiment raised in Wei-hai-wei has proved its devotion to its British officers over and over again. That our system of education is defective may be admitted ; that the sense of duty is more highly developed in Germans than in ourselves must be denied. By their works ye shall know them.

Standard special correspondent (11th October 1900).—WEI-HAI-WEI, 10th August.—. . . It is also gratifying to know that another experiment in connection with Wei-hai-wei, the raising of a Chinese regiment under British officers and non-commissioned officers, has been attended with success. Thanks to the forethought of our high military authorities, it has been proved that Chinese picked from certain parts of the country, and carefully trained by British officers, make excellent fighting material. And the trial has been no light one, when the time available for training for active service, and the circumstances, are remembered. If in the future more should be required, there is little doubt they will be forthcoming; but that they should be willing, as they have now shown they are, to lay down their lives, not for their own country, but for those now fighting against their compatriots, is inexplicable. But China is a land of contradictions, and, now more than ever, of great mysteries.

The Army and Navy Gazette, 29th September 1900.— . . . The *New York Sun* offers some criticism of the Wei-hai-wei regiment on this occasion (the final assault and taking of Tientsin City by the Allies), and says that, though some of the men were raw recruits, all showed what the Chinese can do when well led and well organised. "With the eyes of the fighting men of eight nations watching to see them show the first sign of wavering, they followed their gallant officers with hardly a duck, and swung across that fire-spattered field with almost as much precision as the superb little Japanese." The gallant officers are given great credit for the intrepidity with which they advanced and led their men, but the correspondent of the *Sun* censures them for having "stalked along ahead of the men as unconcerned as if only on parade, instead of helpless under a hell fire of Mannlichers to which they could not reply." The correspondent apparently overlooked the fact that these officers had not only to lead their men, but to do so conspicuously, for it is not likely that the Chinese are yet such trained soldiers that they can recognise the leadership of officers who hide themselves.

North China Daily News, SHANGHAI, 1st September 1900.— (Extract from correspondence from Wei-hai-wei.) . . . There has been a good deal of prejudice against the regiment exhibited in one way and another, largely born of the conviction in many minds that Chinese are no good anyway. Certainly, these prejudices do not seem to have been justified so far. They fought bravely and well under the walls of Tientsin; let it be remembered that they fought with our troops, and on the

o

the side of civilisation and humanity at a time when these abstractions have few friends among the Chinese. It has often been remarked that the Chinese only needed leaders, and the brief history of the Wei-hai-wei regiment confirms this judgment.

The Daily Express, 4th December 1900.—(By Dr Henry Liddell.) . . . There is no doubt that the Chinaman, when properly trained and led by European officers, who will set him a right example in bravery and dash, makes an excellent soldier. Witness the Tae-ping Rebellion and the " 1st Chinese Regiment" of British auxiliary troops, trained by English officers for duty at Wei-hai-wei.

The Daily Graphic, 12th January 1901.—

THE ALLIES IN CHINA.

(By One who was there.)

. . . The Japanese, who are uncommonly shrewd observers, . . . were also much astonished at our Chinese regiment, whose stolid pluck and endurance they could not understand. . . . Before concluding . . . I feel I must make some further reference to that most anomalous corps, the Chinese regiment. The idea of employing Chinese against their own people is one that, as everyone says, would occur to no one but English. The Germans, it is true, tried it once, but their experiment seems to have been a failure, and I believe they are unlikely to repeat it. . . . I have referred to the pluck and endurance of our Chinese, as others have done, but their great utility has escaped general notice, though for good, hard, and useful work they are unexcelled and possibly unequalled. No man is more capable of more physical labour than the ordinary Chinaman, and in his own country this is natural. After Tientsin was taken the Chinese regiment did yeoman service in collecting junks and coolies for the advance on Peking, obtaining for our force a supply of water transport with a facility that was the envy of the other Powers, who had to employ force where we used successfully only persuasion. On the march to Peking, and in

Peking itself, the spectacle of well-fed, contented Chinese did much to conciliate and attract to us the inhabitants of the various districts; and the use these men were to the authorities in many ways, where the most intellectual foreigner would have been at fault, has only to be reflected upon to be fully realised.

The Times, 17th July 1901.— . . . The record of the Chinese regiment is equally remarkable. After two years under their British officers, all but a handful of them volunteered to fight against their own countrymen and the Imperial troops. They were true, without wavering for a moment, to their colours under extraordinarily trying circumstances. They ignored the jeers and the allurements of their own race, and steadily did their duty. The success of our officers in this instance is the more remarkable because it is set off by the failure of the Germans to organise a similar corps. They had devoted about a year to raising a native regiment at Kiao-chau; but, the moment the rank and file learnt upon what errand it was proposed to despatch them, that regiment ceased to exist. After all, there is something in tradition and experience, and in the tact they bring, in the handling of men, and these are advantages, as the events of this year prove, we still possess in a degree which is not only signal but unique.

APPENDIX B

COMPLIMENTARY ORDERS ISSUED WITH REGARD TO THE RELIEF OF THE PEKING LEGATIONS

CHINA EXPEDITIONARY FORCE ORDERS—TUNGCHOW, 13th August 1900.—Sir Alfred Gaselee takes this opportunity of complimenting the troops on the patient pluck and endurance they have displayed on the march from Tientsin to Tungchow. They have experienced most trying heat, but all have done their best, without complaint, and Sir Alfred has every confidence in asking such troops for one great effort more.

The object of their efforts, the relief of the Legations, is almost accomplished, and the General has no doubt that the Queen's soldiers and sailors will display the same courage and endurance in the final struggle that has marked their march.

CHINA EXPEDITIONARY FORCE ORDERS—PEKING, 24th August 1900.—250. The Lieutenant - General commanding has much pleasure in publishing the following telegram from the Secretary of State for India :—

" Her Majesty's Government heartily congratulate you, and request that you will communicate to the officers and men under your command their high appreciation of the skill, courage and endurance shown during the daring advance of the allied forces, and which has been brought to such a successful issue."

CHINA EXPEDITIONARY FORCE ORDERS — PEKING, 27th August 1900.—274. The Lieutenant-General has much pleasure in publishing the following gracious message from Her Majesty The Queen Empress :—

" Heartily congratulate you and all ranks of my troops under your command on the success which has attended your remarkable advance to Peking. Trust that the wounded are doing well. Victoria Regina Imperatrix."

CHINA EXPEDITIONARY FORCE ORDERS—PEKING, 28th August 1900.—283. The Lieutenant-General commanding has much pleasure in publishing the following telegram from His Excellency the Viceroy and Governor-General of India :—

" I congratulate you warmly upon rapid and distinguished success that has attended your movements and upon bravery of all troops under your command."

APPENDIX C

EXTRACTS OF TELEGRAPHIC AND OTHER DESPATCHES

Note.—The telegraphic despatch sent by General Dorward, with reference to the battle of the 27th June 1900, is not reproduced as it was very brief, and its contents, so far as they referred to the Chinese regiment, have been quoted in the text.

From Brigadier-General DORWARD *to* SECRETARY OF STATE FOR WAR.

TIENTSIN, 10*th July*.

Yesterday, 3 A.M., combined force, 1000 Japanese under command of General Fukushima, 550 British troops, 400 British Navy, 100 United States, 400 Russians, under command of myself, attacked enemy's position south-west of city. Positions were quickly captured. Enemy's loss, 350 killed; four small guns. Combined force then attacked Western Arsenal, which, after a short bombardment, was rushed by United States and Japanese. Country west of Arsenal had been flooded by enemy, so no further movement in this direction was possible. Chief object of expedition, which was to clear away guns and enemy to the west of Settlements, completely carried out. Day's honours rested with Japanese and Americans.

Chinese regiment as escort to guns, worked splendidly, getting over difficulties of swampy ground.

From GENERAL OFFICER COMMANDING *North China British Field Force, to the* SECRETARY OF STATE FOR WAR.

TIENTSIN, 11*th July* 1900.

SIR,—I have the honour to submit the following report on the action which took place near here on the 9th inst. :—

2. At 3 A.M., on 9th July, a combined force of Japanese, Russian, American, and British troops moved out from the Taku Gate at the southern end of the foreign Settlements, with the object of clearing the Chinese Imperial troops and Boxers and their guns from the villages south of the Mud Parapet, and also from the Western Arsenal.

3. The force consisted of 1000 Japanese, including three troops of cavalry, a battery of mountain artillery, and a party of engineers, under General Fukushima, and of 950 British (two companies 2nd Battalion Royal Welsh Fusiliers, two 2.5-in. guns, two maxims of the Hong-Kong Royal Artillery, half-company Hong-Kong regiment, two companies 1st Chinese Regiment, 400 Marines and Bluejackets), 400 Russians, and 200 American troops, under my command.

4. The whole force, with the exception of the Americans, who advanced on the Arsenal along the Mud Parapet, proceeded south for one and a half miles by the main road to the village of Tung Lou ; there the force turned to the west, and half-a-mile further on deployed, when opposition from the enemy was met with, the Japanese being on the left and the British troops on the right. The Russians acted as reserve to the British Column.

5. Four guns, that for several days had annoyed the Settlements by their fire from the village of Hei-niu-chuang, were quickly silenced and captured, and the Japanese cavalry were able to execute three successful charges among a considerable body of flying enemy, who had made but slight resistance to our attack.

6. The line then wheeled to the right and attacked the Western Arsenal.

7. The Japanese Engineers had to make a bridge across a small stream before the artillery could advance. The bridge was made under cover of our combined artillery fire, slowly replied to by the enemy's guns left at the Arsenal.

8. At 7.30 A.M. the artillery crossed the stream and took up positions on the further side ; the remainder of the force followed, the left of the line resting on the road leading to the Arsenal and the city. The whole of the country to the west

of the road had been flooded by the enemy and rendered impassable for troops.

9. The Arsenal was quickly captured by a rush of the Japanese and Americans, and was entered at 9 A.M. by the combined forces, which also spread along the Mud Parapet to the west. Artillery was brought up close to the parapet and a heavy fire opened on the city, which was replied to with vigour by the enemy.

10. It had been intended to leave a force to prevent the re-occupation of the Arsenal by the enemy, but, owing to its gutted condition and exposed position, it was considered untenable. The houses surrounding it, which might give cover to guns or snipers, were burned, and the bridge leading to the city from the south destroyed.

11. The combined forces then returned along the Mud Parapet to the Settlements.

12. The success of the attack has relieved our batteries in the British Settlement from both direct and enfilade fire, to which they had been exposed, and has also diminished the number of guns bombarding the Settlements.

13. The most arduous work of the day was done by the Chinese regiment, who, as escort to the guns, worked indefatigably in getting them over broken and swampy country.

14. The casualties in the British force were: one private Royal Welsh Fusiliers, one private Royal Marine Light Infantry, and one Chinese hospital attendant, killed; three privates Royal Welsh Fusiliers, one private Chinese regiment, and one Chinese hospital attendant, wounded. The Americans and Russians had no casualties. The Japanese lost fifty killed and wounded.

15. The Chinese lost 350 killed, and the number of their wounded must been considerable. As a result of the action, General Nieh, one of the best of the Chinese generals, is reported to have been killed or to have committed suicide.—I have, etc.,

A. R. F. DORWARD, Brigadier-General.

From the GENERAL OFFICER COMMANDING BRITISH FORCES, TIENTSIN, *to the* SECRETARY OF STATE FOR WAR

TIENTSIN, 19*th July* 1900.

SIR,—On the afternoon of the 11th inst. I arranged with General Fukushima, commanding the Japanese forces, to carry out as soon as possible the capture of Tientsin City. Owing to our heavy losses during the daily bombardment of the Settlements, we considered this movement necessary.

2. The Russian General was approached on the subject and said he would co-operate in the movement by an attack on the Chinese batteries and fort to the north-east of the city. He desired to get his pontoon-train in readiness, and said that as soon as he had done so he would give me notice of his readiness to move. His staff-officer gave me that notice at 5 P.M. on the 12th inst, and it was arranged that the Russian forces, who had the longer march, should move out in time to deliver their attack about 10 A.M. on the following day, and that the Japanese-British force should deliver their attack on the city as early as possible, in order to attract the bulk of the Chinese troops to their side, and so facilitate the capture of their batteries by the Russians.

3. I then called on Colonel de Pelacot, commanding the French forces, and Colonel Meade, commanding the American forces, and together with them visited General Fukushima to discuss the plan of operations.

4. It was decided that the Allied forces should parade at 3 A.M. and move in three columns—about 500 yards apart—on the Western Arsenal.

5. The French force, 900 strong, was to form the right column, and, crossing the Mud Parapet in the British Extra Concession, was to move on the south side of it, and under its cover, direct on the Arsenal, timing its movement to agree with that of the other columns. Two companies were detailed to advance from the French Settlement and clear the houses between it and the city of troops. They were unable, however, in the face of a heavy fire, to make much headway.

6. The Japanese column, 1500 strong, under General

Fukushima, was to move out from the Settlement by the Racecourse Gate at 3.30 A.M. and move parallel to the Mud Parapet, about 500 yards from it.

7. The left column, consisting of 800 British troops (500 military, and 300 naval), 900 Americans, and 30 Austrians, moved out of the Taku Gate at 3.30 A.M. under my command, and marched parallel to the Japanese column and about 500 yards from them. About 500 yards on the left of the left column were the Japanese cavalry, 150 strong.

8. The left column was somewhat delayed in clearing villages of small parties of the enemy, and its head arrived at the road leading to the Arsenal and South Gate of the city about a quarter of a mile behind the head of the Japanese column.

9. The French column suffered a check at a bridge in the Mud Parapet, about a quarter of a mile from the Arsenal, in crossing over which their troops were exposed to fire. The Arsenal was cleared of the enemy principally through the agency of the Japanese troops.

10. The advanced British troops, consisting of the detachment 2nd Battalion Royal Welsh Fusiliers, and the American Marines, moved forward and lined the Mud Parapet west of the Arsenal, the 9th American Infantry being also brought forward under the parapet as support. The reserve, consisting of two companies of the Chinese regiment and the Naval Brigade, were halted about 2500 yards from the city and suffered some loss from long range fire.

11. All the artillery of the combined force, consisting of mountain guns, with the exception of three 3.2-inch guns belonging to the Americans, formed up a short distance south of the Mud Parapet and bombarded the city. (5-30 A.M.)

12. One 4-inch gun, three 12-prs., and a few 9-prs. and 6-prs., worked by the Navy from a position in the British Extra Concession, did excellent service in keeping down the fire from the city walls.

13. After an hour's bombardment it was decided to attack. The French were to be on the right, the Japanese in the centre, and the British on the left, the centre of the attack being the South Gate. Owing to the attack being pushed on somewhat

too hurriedly in the centre, the Fusiliers and American Marines had to move forward rather too quickly under a heavy fire to get into position on the Japanese left. (7.15 A.M.)

14. General Fukushima had asked me to give some support to the left of his line during the attack, and the 9th American Infantry was directed by me to give this support, and also to support the attack of the Fusiliers and Marines.

15. When the 9th Regiment had crossed the Mud Parapet, a body of men estimated at 1500 strong, made up of cavalry and infantry, appeared about 2500 yards away from our extreme left. I directed the detachment of the Hong-Kong regiment, who up to this time had been acting as escort to the guns, to take up a favourable position at a bend in the Mud Parapet, about one mile from the Arsenal, to meet any attack. They had no difficulty in repulsing this threatened attack with the aid of two Maxim guns sent to assist them as soon as possible.

16. The Japanese attack extended considerably more to the left than had been intended, so that the Fusiliers and Marines were pushed more to the left than had been contemplated, and brought close to heavy enfilade fire from the suburbs south of the south-west corner of the city. They faced that fire in the steadiest way, taking up a position under fairly good cover, and during the whole day prevented a large body of the enemy from making any forward movement.

17. Meanwhile, seven or eight guns of the enemy's artillery were replying to our artillery fire from a fort about one and a quarter miles west of the West Gate of the city.

18. The reserves were ordered up to take cover under the Mud Parapet, and the whole of the artillery moved inside the parapet and took up the best positions obtainable to continue the bombardment.

19. Moving back from the Hong-Kong regiment position I could see nothing of the 9th American Infantry; but when I reached the Arsenal I saw that only a few Japanese troops were extended on the right of the road, and that the French troops were all in compact bodies in the villages on the road leading to the South Gate behind the Japanese, from which I judged that

the fire on the right had been so heavy that the French attacking line could not be formed.

20. At the Arsenal I met the acting Adjutant of the 9th Regiment, who said he had been sent back with news that his regiment were in a very exposed position, which from his description I made out to be near the French Settlement, and that they had lost heavily, their Colonel, amongst others, being mortally wounded. He said he had been ordered to ask for reinforcements, and I directed 100 of the Naval Brigade, under Lieutenant Phillimore, R.N., to proceed to their assistance.

21. I signalled in to Lieutenant-Colonel Bower, who was in command of the forces left in the Settlement, to send me out two more companies of the Chinese regiment, with all the stretchers he could collect; and on their arrival sent the stretchers forward, carried by the men of the regiment, under Major Pereira. Major Pereira made two trips out to the American position and brought back many of their wounded under a very heavy fire, losing several men, and being himself wounded. He told me, on returning from his second trip, that the Americans and the men of the Naval Brigade had got into a fairly safe position, so I decided to leave them there till nightfall. They detained a considerable body of the enemy in front of them, and prevented any attack being made on the right flank of the Japanese.

22. Major Pereira also informed me that the Americans were very badly off for ammunition, so I directed Captain Ollivant and a party of the Chinese regiment to take a further supply to them. While performing this service I regret to say that Captain Ollivant was killed.

23. A Japanese staff officer afterwards told me that he had seen the 9th Regiment moving along the right rear of the Japanese attack in column of fours, and that he was afraid they must have suffered heavy loss.

24. The naval guns were all this time making splendid practice, keeping down the fire from the city walls, and we were anxiously waiting for the sound of the explosion which would tell that the Japanese sappers had reached the city gate and

blown it in. Shortly after 1 P.M. I received the following note from the Japanese chief staff officer :—

"Mon Général,—Nos soldats sont déjà entrés dans la cité. Je vous prie donc de faire cesser le feu de vos canons immédiatement. AOKI, Lieutenant-Colonel."

25. Orders were accordingly given for the cessation of all artillery fire, and the advance of all our troops to support the assault on the city. The advancing troops were met with a very heavy fire from the walls, which continued to increase in intensity, and it soon became apparent that the Japanese troops had not entered the city. The troops were then forced to take cover close to the canal round the city. I shortly afterwards heard from the Japanese general, that he had been misinformed and that his troops had not entered the city.

26. Orders were sent for all guns to open fire again, and owing to the beautiful practice of the naval guns, very little loss was suffered by the troops in the advanced trenches.

27. Towards evening, the 1500 troops on the left flank again advanced and began preparing a long line of shelter trenches. I received a request from General Fukushima, asking me if I could undertake arrangements for the protection of his troops and the French, while in their advanced positions, from attack from the left flank or rear, as his cavalry had informed him that bodies of the enemy were threatening us from those directions.

28. The naval guns were then requested to direct their whole fire on the enemy facing the extreme left of our position, and under cover of that fire and of volleys from the detachment, Hong-Kong regiment, directed on the various points from which the enemy were harassing the retirement, the Fusiliers and American Marines were withdrawn with very slight loss and formed up behind the Mud Parapet. The movement reflected great credit on Colonel Meade, commanding the Marines, and Captain Gwynne, commanding the Fusiliers.

29. The more delicate manœuvre of withdrawing the 9th American Infantry and the company of the Naval Brigade had then to be undertaken. The naval guns were directed to sweep

the barriers constructed along the fringe of houses between the French Settlement and the city, from which the fire on the American troops proceeded. The American troops themselves were only about 300 yards from this fringe, and there was great danger of the fire from the naval guns injuring them as well as the enemy. The dead and wounded, of which the Americans had still a considerable number with them, were brought back with the assistance of the company of the Naval Brigade, and shortly afterwards the 9th Regiment arrived at the Mud Parapet in safety. I would specially bring to notice the conduct of Major Jesse Lee during the retirement; in him his regiment possesses an officer of exceptional merit.

30. The whole force is under the greatest obligation to Captain Bayly and Lieutenant Drummond, Royal Navy, for their working of the naval guns.

31. After posting troops to secure our flank and rear from attack, the troops turned in for the night, during which there was some rain.

32. About 3 A.M. next day the Japanese sappers, crossing the canal by a bridge they had made during the night, blew in the South Gate, and in less than an hour, after some desultory street-fighting, the city was in our possession.

33. The British force seized a number of junks and one small steamer on the canal north of the city, which will be useful when we advance on Pekin, and also the eight guns which had kept up a steady fire on our artillery throughout the previous day.

34. News was then received that the Russian attack on the other side of the city had been delayed by unforeseen causes, but when made had proved very successful, resulting in the complete rout of the Chinese and the capture of 11 guns; the Russian loss was about 120 killed and wounded.

35. The losses of the Allied forces in the attack on the South Gate were as follows:—

Royal Marine Light Infantry.—Killed, Captain Lloyd; slightly wounded, Major Luke; wounded, 16 men.

Royal Navy.—Slightly wounded, Lieutenant Field; killed, 5 men; wounded, 19 men.

Royal Welsh Fusiliers.—Killed, 5 men ; wounded, 12 men.

Hong-Kong regiment.—Wounded, 8 men, of whom 1 afterwards died.

Hong-Kong companies, Royal Artillery.—Killed, 2 men ; wounded, 5 men.

Chinese regiment. — Killed, Captain Ollivant; slightly wounded, Major Pereira, and 1 European non-commissioned officer ; killed, 5 men ; wounded, 13 men, of whom 1 afterwards died.

American forces.—9th Infantry,—Colonel Liscum and 22 men killed, 3 officers and 70 men wounded. Marines, 5 killed, and 27 wounded.

French forces.—110 killed and wounded.

Japanese forces.—400 killed and wounded.

Austrians.—5 wounded.

. . . .

43. Captain Watson, of the Chinese regiment, led his men well, and the two companies with him were among the first troops to enter the city. He has specially brought to my notice the conduct of No. 94 Sergeant Chi-dien-kwei, who was in command of a half-company without any European.

44. The artillery, under Major St John, was very well handled, and managed to make their ammunition last considerably longer than the artillery of the other nations did. As they were firing black powder, they were at a distinct disadvantage with the artillery of the enemy, who were using smokeless powder, thus rendering the exact location of their guns very difficult.

. . . .

I have, etc.,
A. R. F. DORWARD, Brigadier-General.

From SIR A. GASELEE, *General Officer Commanding China Expeditionary Force, to the* SECRETARY OF STATE FOR INDIA.

No. 36S. HEADQUARTERS, CHINA EXPEDITIONARY FORCE, PEKING, 19*th August* 1900.

MY LORD,—Now that the first and paramount duty of relieving the Legations has been successfully performed, I am in a position to address to your Lordship a preliminary Despatch, describing the operations of the British forces in Northern China from the 27th July, the date on which I arrived at Tientsin, to the 14th August, the date on which we entered Peking.

2. On my arrival at Tientsin I at once put myself into communication with the general officers commanding the American and Japanese forces, and soon came to a satisfactory understanding with them. We decided to collectively impress on the Allied commanders the absolute necessity of pressing forward towards Peking at the earliest possible moment, and, happily, our views were eventually accepted.

At a conference held on the 3rd August, it was arranged to commence the advance on the 4th, with approximately 20,000 men—viz.

> 10,000 Japanese, with 24 guns.
> 4000 Russians, with 16 guns.
> 3000 British, with 12 guns.
> 2000 Americans, with 6 guns.
> 800 French, with 12 guns.
> 200 Germans.
> 100 Austrians and Italians.
>
> ------
>
> 20,100, with 70 guns.

4. In pursuance of the above agreement, the British troops (marginally noted) moved from Tientsin to Hsi-ku on the afternoon of the 4th, and bivouacked. . . . . The British were followed by the Americans and Japanese, who bivouacked. . .

Naval Brigade, 4 guns.
Royal Marine Light Infantry, 300.
12th Battery, Royal Field Artillery, 6 guns.
Hong-Kong Artillery, 2 guns, 4 maxims.
Detachment, Royal Engineers.
1st Bengal Lancers, 400.
Royal Welsh Fusiliers, 300.
7th Bengal Infantry, 500.
24th Punjab Infantry, 300.
1st Sikh Infantry, 500.

Hong-Kong Regiment, 100.
Chinese Regiment, 100.

.   .   .   .

I have, etc.,
ALFRED GASELEE, *Lieutenant-General,*
Commandng China Expeditionary Force.

From LIEUTENANT-GENERAL SIR ALFRED GASELEE,
Commanding British Contingent, China Expeditionary Force.
PEKING, 17*th January* 1901.

.   .   .   .   .   .

It is now my pleasing duty to bring to Your Lordship's notice those officers whose duties have been performed in such a manner as to call for my recognition.

.   .   .   .

First Chinese Regiment.—A detachment of the regiment was present on the march to Peking, and afterwards did well on the lines of communication. The services of Captain A. A. S. Barnes call for recognition.

.   .   .   .

Lines of Communication.—The following officers on the lines of communication in their various capacities have rendered good service :—

.   .   .   .   .   .

Major (local Lieutenant-Colonel) H. Bower, Commanding 1st Chinese Regiment, and Captain (local Major) G. H. G. Mockler, I.S.C., have done excellent service in the civil administration of Tientsin, the one as a member of the Provisional Government, and the other as Chief of Police.

Note.—Only those portions of the above Despatches actually referring to the regiment, or throwing any light on the operations in which it took part, and which form a portion of my narrative of these events, are here reproduced.

P

APPENDIX D

LIST OF CASUALTIES SUSTAINED BY THE CHINESE REGIMENT IN NORTH CHINA, JUNE TO OCTOBER 1900

KILLED.

Captain L. O. E. Ollivant, killed in action, 13th July 1900.

Captain A. J. Hill, died of injuries received at Tungchow, 18th September 1900.

No. 593 Private Yu-yung-hua, died of wounds received in action at Tientsin railway station, 4th July 1900.

No. 751 Private Ma-ming-chen, killed in action of 6th July 1900.

No. 846 Private Kan-yung-shun, killed in action of 6th July 1900.

No. 507 Private Chau-te-yin, killed in capture of Tientsin City 13th July 1900.

No. 428 Private Hsu-chang-sheng, killed in capture of Tientsin City, 13th July 1900.

No. 363 Private Kuan-wei-ting, killed in capture of Tientsin City, 13th July 1900.

No. 672 Private Liu-fu-yung, killed in capture of Tientsin City, 13th July 1900.

No. 461 Private Liang-hung-en, killed in capture of Tientsin City, 13th July 1900.

No. 893 Private Tsung-te-gung, drowned in the Peiho, 21st July 1900.

No. 597 Private Liang-liu, drowned in the Peiho, 8th August 1900.

No. 5 Sergeant Chi-dien-kwei, killed at Tungchow, 15th September 1900.

No. 678 Interpreter Li-yi-fan, killed at Tungchow, 15th September 1900.

226

No. 261 Private Liu-te-sheng, killed at Tungchow, 15th September 1900.

No. 309 Private Liu-pei-lan, killed at Tungchow, 15th September 1900.

No. 430 Private Li-ssu, killed at Tungchow, 15th September 1900.

No. 427 Private Yang-yung-shen, killed at Tungchow, 15th September 1900.

No. 690 Sung-cheng-an, killed at Tungchow, 15th September 1900.

No. 714 Private Wang-hsung-tai, killed at Tungchow, 15th September 1900.

No. 726 Private Sha-pau-te, killed at Tungchow, 15th September 1900.

No. 460 Lance-Corporal Wei-ting-hsu, killed on convoy duty on the Peiho, 6th September 1900.

No. 924 Private Chang-hung-an, killed near Ho-hsi-wu, 24th September 1900.

WOUNDED.

Major C. D. Bruce, shot through the liver, 6th July 1900.

Major G. Pereira, slightly, at capture of Tientsin City.

Colour-Sergeant R. Purdon, shot through the leg at capture of city.

No. 152 Bombardier Li-ping-chen, shell wound in thigh at Tientsin railway station, 4th July 1900.

No. 462 Private Chau-lien-sheng, bullet wound in left leg at railway station, 4th July 1900.

No. 606 Private Tsau-shih-ching, shell wound in stomach at Hai-kwan-ssu Arsenal, 9th July 1900.

No. 99 Lance-Sergeant Yi-pin, bullet wound, right shoulder, 13th July 1900.

No. 85 Private Han-shou-chan, bullet wound, right arm, 13th July 1900.

No. 86 Private Yang-shih-tung, bullet wound, right leg, 13th July 1900.

No. 431 Private Su-te-sheng, bullet wound, right breast and arm, 13th July 1900.

No. 524 Private Wang-tsung-ho, bullet wound, abdomen, 13th July 1900.

No. 337 Corporal Hsu-ting-fa, bullet wound, arm and hip, 13th July 1900.

No. 302 Lance-Corporal Li-fu-yi, bullet wound, right shoulder and right side, 13th July 1900.

No. 236 Private Hsu-te-sheng, bullet wound, left shoulder, 13th July 1900.

No. 842 Private Chin-tso-hsun, shell wounds in both legs, 6th July 1900.

No. 880 Private Tung-wu-ching, shell wounds in shoulder, 6th July 1900.

No. 257 Lance-Corporal Tsau-feng-mau, burned at Tungchow, 15th September 1900.

No. 686 Private Chi-lau-ho, burned at Tungchow, 15th September 1900.

Note.—There were at least five more men wounded at the taking of Tientsin City; but, owing to the rapidity with which they recovered, it is not now possible to give their names, but their injuries were probably only slight.

It should be stated that the total strength of the regiment that went to the front was, all told: 14 officers, 8 British non-commissioned officers, and 363 Chinese non-commissioned officers and men, so that our percentage of losses was very high.

Lightning Source UK Ltd.
Milton Keynes UK
UKOW050605180512

192793UK00001B/45/P